AF235696

GETTING THAT **EXPAT** JOB

IN INTERNATIONAL DEVELOPMENT

AND ADVANCING

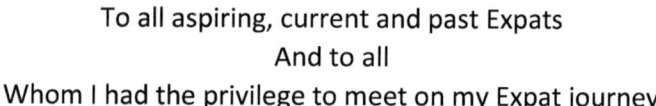
To all aspiring, current and past Expats
And to all
Whom I had the privilege to meet on my Expat journey

MIX
Papier aus verantwortungsvollen Quellen
Paper from responsible sources
FSC® C105338

FSC
www.fsc.org

GETTING THAT **EXPAT** JOB

IN INTERNATIONAL DEVELOPMENT

AND ADVANCING

J. F. Loeber

Bibliographical Information of the German National Library / Bibliografische Information der Deutschen Nationalbibliothek: Die Deutsche Nationalbibliothek verzeichnet diese Publikation in der Deutschen Nationalbibliografie; detaillierte bibliografische Daten sind im Internet über dnb.dnb.de abrufbar.

© 2022 J. F. Loeber
All rights reserved
Frankfurt/M Metropolitan Area, Germany

Related website: www.xpatjobsupport.com
Contact: info@xpatjobsupport.com

Production and Publisher / Herstellung und Verlag:
BoD – Books on Demand, Norderstedt, Germany

ISBN 9783756295593

Table of Contents

Acknowledgements: For publishing guidance I am most indebted to BoD – Books on Demand, and for images used or integrated in the book (pp. 100, 124, 131, 141, 159, 161, 163, 164), most grateful for the resources at pixabay.com.

Disclaimers: No liability is assumed for external links and respective websites/contents, including any damage occurring from such. Third-party owners are responsible for their websites; the author of this book has no influence on linked external websites.

In this book the author does not provide legal advice, professional healthcare or similar other professional advice, nor act as an attorney, healthcare or similar professional, and assumes no liability in such or other regard. All examples/instances cited are fictional unless referenced otherwise. All content is provided noncommittally and solely represents general information and/or views, presented only for educational, informational, research and review purposes and/or for purposes of serving the public good, assisting individuals/professionals in or interested in international development in obtaining knowledge and awareness to support them in their career and effectiveness on the ground.

P A R T 1

_____ CHAPTER 1 _____

Scope of this book

You've always wanted to work at an international organisation such as the United Nations (UN), the European Commission, a European Union (EU) Agency, another intergovernmental organisation or an NGO in international development and/or you want to move ahead in it or another organisation ? Congratulations, then this is the right book for you ! No matter for what type of position, at what level or in which area.

I will be giving you hands-on, practical advice, based on experience, reflection and review. Less scientific, but real and usable, for immediate application.

This book is for all the diligent, dedicated people, collaborating in collegial spirit to improve peoples' lives in the realization of (sustainable) development goals. It does not address ways of deceiving, colluding, manipulating and other objectionable methods of getting into or moving ahead in a system. This exists in places and there is literature on these ways, but this is not the perspective of this book. The basic premise here is that the respective system is good and functioning and you will both survive and flourish within or outside its boundaries.

The book is divided into two parts: Part 1 is on job application strategies, procedures and securing that new job, and Part 2 is on starting, staying and advancing in that new job. While Part 1 relates in many respects to processes and practice at the UN, the European Commission, EU Agencies, other intergovernmental organisations, donors/International Financial Institutions (IFIs), NGOs and similar major development institutions, Part 2 and its on-the-job recommendations are based on and apply to the broad spectrum of public institutions, both international and national, the not-for-profit sector (NGOs), public-private ventures and ideally also the corporate/private sector.

With that, let's get started !

****

_____ CHAPTER 2 _____

What do you want and where do you want to go?

In starting out on this project in your life, it is important to be clear in your mind what you are seeking.

What is your preferred area of work ? What is your main field, what are the auxiliary field(s) ? What are some outlier areas, fanciful and yet not impossible ? What are some of

> ❖ *Disaster Management*
> ❖ *Communication*
> ❖ *Conference Services*
> ❖ *Technology*
> ❖ *Trade and Commerce*
> ❖ *Political Affairs*
> ❖ *Law, Human Rights*
> ❖ *Humanitarian Aid*
> ❖ *Human Resources*
> ❖ *Administration*
> ...

Table 1 Preferred work areas

these way out areas, areas that you dream of, but near enough that with some experience and/or training, they can become within reach ? More broadly, what is your purpose ? Dare to think big, be audacious !

What type of position are you currently working in, and at what level ? Are you a support staff, a professional, an expert, an executive ?

At which stage of your career do you currently find yourself: novice, mid-career, senior / seasoned staff, post-career ?

Do you have preference for any specific Organisation, a Specialized Agency or associated institution in the larger Organisation / Institution ? Would you exclude some specific ones or parts (e.g. ones you cannot identify with or which you have previously worked at) ? There are e.g. some 100 organisations, funds, specialised agencies and other entities and related organisations just in the UN system [1]!

Do you have preference for a particular location(s) ? Which location(s) would you exclude right from the start ? Are you willing to go to unstable areas of the world, conflict zones ?[2]

---

[1] See the chart and list at
http://www.un.org/en/aboutun/structure/pdfs/UN_System_Chart_2015_Rev.4_ENG_11x17colour.pdf and
http://www.unsceb.org/directory.

[2] Note that some positions may initially appear more dangerous than they are in reality, as conflicts/hazards may be limited to specific areas and times. Since the reverse is also possible, e.g. endemic cardiovascular disease or other prevalent condition in a

What type and level of position are you aspiring to, in the short- and long-term ? What are your larger goals, specifically and more broadly ? Again, dare and think big ! This is about you.

Are you seeking project-type work or a functional position ?

Are you seeking a temporary, fixed-term or indefinite engagement ? Unfortunately, today indefinite contracts are more rare at many organisations and increasingly becoming extinct. But flexibility also means opportunity !

There are also job openings for rostered positions, i.e. positions that materialize at a later date, to be filled by rostered candidates.

Here's a checklist for your current situation and preferences:

****

---

population, sound research and objective information gathering are in any case advisable.

Vision 1 ½ – 2 years ahead	
Current position	*Communications Associate*
Level	G-6
Desired position	*Human Resources Officer*
Level	P-3
Area	Human Resources
Preferred organisation(s)	-
Excluded organisation(s)	ABC
Preferred location(s)	Vienna
Excluded location(s)	Hotspot conflict zones

Table 2 Vision looking ahead

_____ CHAPTER 3 _____

Planning

While managing your career is a full-time job and requires your attention 24/7, it makes sense to organise job planning in manageable segments. You need a life too ! Make a concentrated effort, with an end date in sight.

In larger organisations it can take some 6 – 12 months to get a new job, sometimes longer (15 - 24 months), rarely shorter. This is counting from the time you decide to get that new job until you have signed the contract and are sitting in your new office. Spontaneous, short-term job opportunities are rare or short-lived, and mostly just wishful thinking.

Having been in a position for a longer time and worked hard, many will expect to be acknowledged and promoted/ rewarded some time. However, there is no guarantee of a career in places such as the UN. Normally, what you see is what you get. You therefore have to be the master of your own destiny and create your own opportunities and then take them as they materialize.

Therefore you need to plan ahead and start early. Make your resolution to get that new job by the middle or end of next year !

Over a period of, let's say, 1 ½ years, plan to write dozens and dozens of applications, sit maybe some 5 – 15 written tests, be invited to some 3 – 6 interviews and get 1 – 3 job offers. That may sound too much or too little, but it's what could be realistic. But admittedly this is not universally applicable and definitely not cast in stone - set your own targets, gather experience, validate them and adjust your planning as you see fit. The important part is to buy into and own your career planning.

Good general resources are:

❖ development aid
https://www.developmentaid.org/#!/jobs/search

❖ devex
https://www.devex.com/jobs/search/

❖ reliefweb
https://reliefweb.int/jobs

For opportunities at the EU, recommendable are:

❖ https://epso.europa.eu/job-opportunities_en

❖ https://eeas.europa.eu/headquarters/headquarters-homepage/area/jobs-funds_en

❖ https://ec.europa.eu/international-partnerships/jobs_en

❖ https://euagencies.eu/jobs/job-vacancy-list

❖ https://www.coe-recruitment.com/index.aspx

Entry points for careers in the UN are:

❖ https://hr.un.org/ and

❖ https://careers.un.org/lbw/Home.aspx

❖ https://unjoblist.org

If it's difficult to land a job in your dream organisation, seeking an engagement as a consultant, volunteer (e.g. UN Volunteers, https://www.unv.org/) or spending an internship (paid or unpaid), in order to have a foot in the door, may be a good idea. However, this also comes with some risk (moving e.g. from a salaried position to a consultancy engagement) and/or financial loss (unpaid internship). Therefore, it may be better to seek out temporary positions, which are increasingly advertised in an increasingly short-lived labour market. The potential transition to a fixed position can in any case be easier. At the workplace, one is thereby almost a regular employee – some individuals may hold multiple successive temporary contracts over the years, spanning almost a whole career, with mandatory contract breaks (e.g. for a month after a two year period).

****

_____ CHAPTER 4 _____

CV, Cover letter and Q&As

<u>CV</u>

A crucial first step in your preparations is writing up / revising your CV (curriculum vitae). This is important, as much of the screening for short listing is done based on the CV, sometimes in automated processes (AI). CV forms vary, for the EU there is e.g. the popular EU Pass CV, https://europa.eu/europass/en. The UN CV and online profiles are based on the traditional UN Personal History Form, in use for many years and still available e.g. at http://www.uneca.org/pages/vacancies. Many institutions have their own type of CV form or variant and make it compulsory to use it, even if it basically has very similar information fields. This is annoying, but unavoidable.

Sometimes vacancies also allow for sending in a CV – this can be on a form of your preference. For a traditional organisation, it will be preferable to keep that form similar to those in that sector. When dealing with an innovative, agile organisation, following a new CV standard format will be recommendable, comprising a) maximum two pages headlining experience, education and training/skills, pre-pended by b) a page with a picture and bullet points highlighting key qualifications, and appended by c) one or more pages of activities, grouped by subject/theme.

A good CV will take about 3 – 4 days to prepare. Take care and do brainstorming to be sure to include everything relevant. In their preliminary check, Human Resources Departments will search for evidence of experience and oftentimes specific key words mentioned in the vacancy notice, or related words, and as mentioned such screening could also be done in automated processes. Besides identifying, naming and including your core and main qualifications, be sure to include also activities which you have supported, helped with, even and perhaps particularly those on an ad hoc basis. Sometimes those are just the very ones demonstrating the experience needed for your new position ! E.g. did you substitute or participate in an important committee, while your colleague(s) were on leave ? Did you add to a report from another department ? Think about it - it will pay off for advancing and/or a lateral move.

Recruitment e-portals may require entering all information online, essentially generating a CV. Unfortunately, this is frequent and it is annoying to re-enter information again and again. However, even within organisations there is not necessarily conformity and/or transferability of data, reflecting lacking coherence. The process may take a few hours and therefore preparation and planning ahead is critical. Ideally, it will be possible to replicate information from your existent, completed CV forms, bringing the time input down to 1 or 1 ½ hours. Naturally it is best/economical to avoid double work and/or inconsistencies between documents. Having a table at the ready with your exact employment and education dates (from – to), as well as data, information on your various trainings and certificates (title, date(s), place, organiser/institution) will be very helpful too.

To make matters worse, requirements for data fields - minimum/maximum size of text entries - can vary too, in particular for entering previous work experience. Such fields can e.g. be from 1000 up to 5000 characters each. The fields may also be divided up into "duties" and "activities", with separate text limitations for each. My advice would be to pre-prepare with a standard overall length of 1500 characters, with 500 characters for the duties, and 1000 characters for the activities. Formulate the text in a generic way, and aim to structure it into modules which can be compounded, e.g. general module(s) followed by specific (additional/alternative) ones, covering specific activities as relevant and/or if overall more than 1500 characters space is available.

When, on the other hand, encountering a 1000 character overall text limitation for an experience data field, editing/shortening will be required. Hopefully that will not take too long, as shortening text is generally easier than lengthening text. The derived text version can then be stored as an alternative for future applications with that same text limitation. For experience dating back some five years or more, it may in any case be advisable from the start to keep to a 1000 character standard text entry, with about 300 characters for duties and 700 characters for activities.

Qualifications and training may be entered with differing details or categorised in different ways too. This can be a real challenge for applicants and frankly, sometimes quite a nightmare. But, until e.g. "One UN" is realised, EU coherence advances respectively, or a uniform approach is generally taken in the development sector, introducing harmonised recruitment, one will have to live with these circumstances. My recommendation is therefore to just remain calm and patient. With some practice, a new profile can be completed increasingly quickly, sometimes maybe even just under an hour.

> *Aim for **1500 characters** text for each job description, with **500 characters** for duties and **1000 characters** for activities*

Table 3 Text length recommendation per job entry

Pay attention to highlighting your achievements in concrete, understandable ways, e.g. "about 50 tenders executed", "about 500 purchase orders approved", "turnover of 20 mn US$" or "20 workshops held". Where you are not sure, estimate. While the CV should not be a mathematical or overall vociferous exercise, concrete figures or descriptions will help to substantiate performance and allow you to shine as merited.

<u>Cover letter</u>

The cover letter (motivation letter) is similarly tricky, as requirements can vary. In particular, the maximum length can typically range between 1000 and 5000 characters, and occasionally also be unlimited. My recommendation would be to work with a basic text of some 3500 characters (about one page with 5 – 6 paragraphs), supplemented by, if desired and not already appended to the CV (new type format), an optional annex with activities/examples under specific headings/competencies (e.g. Public Health Sector experience, Systems experience, training). Though if in doubt I would recommend to do without the annex, as it may quickly become information overload and detract from the main text and readability.

If you have worked in several positions, try to group or consolidate this experience by job type or family. What is in the CV does not need to be repeated and/or enumerated.

The text should again be built up modularly, with general wording that can be supplemented by specific modules according to requirements. E.g. the general text could say *"With postings at the UN and international NGOs over a period of more than 10 years, I have gained in-depth knowledge and understanding of international development work, both in expert and leadership functions. Complex operations overseen by myself include leading field missions, emergency response and donor coordination."*

A subsequent, specific module could then detail *"Emergency, humanitarian response and post-conflict activities have included coordination support for the ABC Project in Sudan following unrests; implementing a temporary shelter programme in Sri Lanka with XYZ after the 2021 floods; supporting civil society engagement with the DEF Institute in Kosovo in 2008 after its declaration of independence."* Or, in a cover letter e.g. on procurement / supply chain, supplementary modules could be on organising stakeholder meetings with supply chain actors, and/or contributing to Sustainable Development Goals (SDGs) / Corporate Social Responsibility (CSR) through procurement actions.

From the 3500 characters, it is possible to both condense the text to e.g. 1000 or 2000 characters, or to expand it via modules to 4000 – 5000 characters. Note in this regard e.g. that the UN standard motivation letter, previously allowing for about 5000 characters, is now limited to 2000 characters[3]. This appears to be due to introduction of specific Q&As (questionnaires) at the outset of the application.

The cover letter can be structured into:
- ❖ General background, qualifications;
- ❖ Brief consolidated experience;
- ❖ Relevant functional experience and competencies;
- ❖ Requirements for the position <u>and</u> how these are met (congruency / matching);
- ❖ Voluntary activities / relevant training;

---

[3] Application process under
https://careers.un.org/lbw/home.aspx?lang=en-US.

- ❖ Overall reason and motivation for applying;
- ❖ Optional annex with details / data.

Overleaf is a sample structure of a cover letter of about 1800 characters length

Of course the cover letter should ideally be fully tailored to the position, matching experience, qualifications etc. and outlining understanding of the position and how you would be able to add value to it and contribute to the organisation's objectives. However, unfortunately positions may sometimes be pre-orientated to an incumbent or other associated person, so that a fair and objective process may not be guaranteed[4]. It is at times impossible to know what the real chances for a position are. And the complaint route will be arduous, as proof of any irregularity is normally hard to come by, besides risking being perceived as a grouser before you have even ever set foot in the new organisation.

Nevertheless, on the positive side, processes may evolve differently than expected for any number of internal and external reasons, so there will likely for the most part be a real chance of securing the advertised position. And there are many positions where suitably qualified candidates are absolutely truly needed due to the specific demands and context of the job. Altogether it would seem therefore that a

---

[4] Browse jurisprudence on this at e.g.
https://www.un.org/en/internaljustice/undt/judgments-orders.shtml;
https://www.ilo.org/dyn/triblex/triblexmain.advancedSearch?p_lang=en.

This position with XYZ has captured my particular interest.

With over ten years' experience in the development sector and backed by degrees in public policy and communication, I have extensive expertise in core areas of humanitarian aid and coordination, policy development, outreach and … . Given this background I possess the necessary skills, qualifications and drive to execute emergency coordination functions at senior institutional levels. This applies both on a broader level, such as strategy development, stakeholder coordination, advocacy … and on specific levels in terms of …

The holistic approach described as critical for this position I believe is strongly reflected in the above experience and implemented activities, such as ABC. Concerning the additional aspect of resource mobilization, demonstrating also results orientation and professionalism, I can refer to my successful interaction with the Foundation for Democracy, helping to secure a 1 mn US$ grant for rule of law programmes in DEF, as well as with Corporate Social Responsibility programmes of companies in the LMN sector, securing donations in kind.

My professional activities have been supplemented by voluntary ones, such as election coordination for the JKL Association and Editorial Adviser for the Election Compendium. Prior to my deployments in [location / region] I have undergone specialized training in electoral assistance and rule of law programmes.

~~For a summary of relevant activities, please see the listing in the attached Annex.~~ (Optional)

I have previously engaged with XYZ in a joint mission to [location] and have been convinced of its efficiency in project implementation, particularly through its cost recovery business model. In the new function I would be able to add value through project milestone tracking techniques which I helped develop and presented [or learned / acquired] at the recent NN Humanitarian Conference in Valencia, Spain.

Given this background and motivated to take on a new challenge, I would be most enthusiastic to work in the advertised position, contributing to reaching XYZ's goals.

Table 4 Example cover letter

reasonable balance needs to be struck between effort and reality. In practice this would mean to work with a generic cover letter, supplemented by specific modules as needed, and reserve the tailor-made cover letter from time to time for "dream" or very fitting positions, and for which there is no immediate, certain indication of any pre-determination, i.e. a reasonable chance on principle of potentially securing the position.

Take care to file all your CVs, individual cover letters and modules for easy and fast access and replication/modification. Choose a system that works for you, e.g. sorted by work area, subject/theme, possibly subdivided by institution type, text length. Here is a sample folder structure:

- ☐ Cover 1000 char
- ☐ Cover 3500 char
    - ☐ Administration
    - ☐ Communication
    - ☐ Customer Service
    - ☐ Emergency, Crisis Mgmt
    - ☐ Field
    - ☐ HR
    - ☐ Language – FR
    - ☐ Language - SP
    - ☐ Modules
    - ☐ Outreach
    - ☐ Programme Mgmt
    - ☐ Resource Mobilization

Table 5 Sample folder structure for cover letters

Q&As

Q&As at the start of application entry forms (e.g. at EU, UN) can be a lot of work, as these require tailoring. Standard text fields can be 1000 (e.g. UN[5]) or 2000 if not 4000 characters (e.g. some EU institutions), or from 100 to 500 words. There can be few (2 – 3) questions, or even up to a dozen or more. Important is to plan your answers and pace yourself, ideally well ahead of the application deadline. E.g. foreseeing a schedule of doing two questions per morning / afternoon, i.e. four questions per day, seems reasonable and without risking to overburden oneself.

It is also recommendable to prepare answers offline, not only to avoid the stress of developing texts in real time in pre-determined text boxes, but also to avoid the risk of being cut out with unsaved text due to expiry of the application system's timelock or internet connection interruption. Therefore, copy-paste questions into a blank text file for preparing answers. Indeed, nothing can be more frustrating than losing text due to being locked out ! Yet, if this really does happen - and it has happened to me - a tip in that situation: Try to set the anguish aside, pause just for a short moment, and then immediately set about re-developing the text, while still fresh in consciousness.

And on developing texts in general – while this may seem old-fashioned - pen/pencil and paper may still be the best tool and actually ultimately outperform direct text input onto the screen. Sketching out ideas and concepts first on

---

[5] https://careers.un.org/lbw/home.aspx?lang=en-US

paper (or ipad/tablet), including arrows, pointers and bubbles, and even writing out a first draft by hand, are essential and valuable, if not indispensable steps. The final text will oftentimes come much quicker this way, flowing more naturally to its final form, without major adjustments, text shifts or corrections, and actually therefore become an overall time-saver.

Answers which are specific and information-rich will be concrete in terms of setting out experience, qualifications, knowledge, supported by dates / data, organisations, locations, matching the posed question. With the limited text space available, grouping experience (e.g. programme management experience gained across a range of institutions, countries/regions) is a very good idea. Short or cryptic answers without providing appreciable specifics, giving the impression of having been set down in a rush, will regularly be scored less, or be invalidated or may even lead to exclusion from the recruitment process altogether.

It is very recommendable also to establish a good e-filing system (repository) for all answers provided to such Q&A, sorted by theme/subject/area, basically similar to the cover letters and/or its various specific modules. Thankfully over time, on the other hand, questions in application e-templates will appear to start repeating themselves or be quite similar, so that it should increasingly be possible to draw on the repository for answers, oftentimes with minimal adjustment, thereby significantly reducing time input and efforts in completing this part of applications.

****

_____ CHAPTER 5 _____

Identifying job opportunities

To find that job, you will have to go about it systematically. Yes, colleagues and friends may inform you about opportunities, and you should definitely keep up as a general matter of principle with all your positive acquaintances. But the information may unfortunately lastly be neither complete nor timely.

It's best to visit search engines regularly and sign up for their email alerts. Some common search engines as partially mentioned above are:

- Devex https://www.devex.com/jobs
- DevelopmentAid
  https://www.developmentaid.org/#!/jobs/search
- reliefweb http://reliefweb.int/jobs
- Global Careers Fair
  https://www.globalcareersfair.com/job-board/
- EU https://epso.europa.eu/job-opportunities_en
- EU https://euagencies.eu/jobs/job-vacancy-list
- UN careers https://careers.un.org/lbw/Home.aspx
- UNjobs http://unjobs.org/

- UNjobfinder https://unjobfinder.org/
- UN Job List https://unjoblist.org/
- ICSC jobnet https://jobs.unicsc.org/

For the UN, the UN Job List e.g. is practical – it can be tailored to position type / level, agency, location and keywords. You can save the webpage with your details / preferences, for refreshing online whenever needed, and receive alerts.

As a standard rule I would recommend to go through these search engines on a weekly basis or every two weeks. Ideally, you should view your favourite few engines every 2 - 3 days or even daily. Some positions are only published for a short time - the minimum period I have seen is six calendar days. Some institutions may not be captured by the search engines – for these direct visits of their websites[6] will be necessary.

From your periodic review of search engines / websites, you can prepare a list of job opportunities, valid for about 2 – 6 weeks, listing in reverse chronological order by due date the position, level, location, source (search engine) and institution. Then, each day you only need to consult the list and act on the ones at the very top, i.e. with upcoming (ideally 2 – 3 days in advance) or same day application due dates. See the example on the next page.

---

[6] For individual EU institutions, see e.g. the search engine at https://european-union.europa.eu/institutions-law-budget/institutions-and-bodies/institutions-and-bodies-profiles_en. For the UN, see e.g. links and references at https://careers.un.org/lbw/home.aspx?viewtype=WWD and https://unsceb.org/.

Position	Organisation	Location	Level	Source	Comment	Deadline
HR Officer	ENV Now	Nairobi	Senior	DEVEX	New NGO	15/04/22
Programme Officer	European Commission DG X	Brussels	AD 7	EPSO	Actual deadline 18/04/22, 5 Q&As	16/04/22
Communica-tion Officer	UNICEF	Copenhagen	P-3	UNICEF		17/04/22
Training Officer	ADB	Manila	Senior	development aid	Actual deadline 20/04/22 16.00 h local time	19/04/22
Training Officer	EU Agency X	Stockholm	FG IV	UN Job List		21/04/22
Senior Career Development Officer	FAO	Rome	P-4	reliefweb		25/04/22
...						

Table 6 Example list of job opportunities

Getting that new job requires a concentrated effort, best daily, sending off some 1 – 2 applications a day. Yes, that's right, ideally daily ! Probably evenings will be best for this, but beware of a) some positions (EU sometimes) closing at midday or close of business 17.00 h and b) time zones and that e.g. Asian positions may be closing earlier if you are located westwards. For these positions and in any case due to possibly voluminous application e-questionnaires, it is best to highlight them accordingly and/or pre-mark them 2 – 3 days earlier in your list of opportunities.

About 1 - 2 applications a day may sound like a lot, but I can promise that once you get into the routine, it is indeed do-able and maybe even fun. Trade in the couch, daydreaming and typing on your mobile phone or tablet and/or consuming or aimlessly surfing the internet for truly investing in your life, with a few dispatched applications. What a great and rewarding way to finish the day !

If your work week is very tight, you can try to shift most applications or important ones to the prior weekend. This particularly goes for those tailored cover letters and specific Q&As, or if/when you need to update your CV and/or other material.

Or, as a minimum, write yourself alerts (post-its or e-alerts) so that you do not forget deadlines for important positions during the week. It's happened to me, missing a range of vacancy deadlines because of travel or impending travel. What a bummer ! In future, better be safe than sorry. Avoid those avoidable regrets, as they can get you down and really persist for long periods !

_____ CHAPTER 6 _____

Table of Competencies

After you have set your job position-tracker(s) in motion, start to work on your Table of Competencies with examples from your past achievements/challenges. You will need this for interviews and you don't want to be caught cold without this tool. Many interviews are competency-based, or at least partially so. As you may need to invest quite some time in the table, including researching and reflecting diligently on your past activities, it is best to start as early as possible with this exercise. The positive side is that the table will remain valid and support your interviews for years to come.

I suggest the following steps for the table:

1) Establish the core competencies applicable to most jobs within your interest (e.g. analysis, strategic thinking, judgement, …), as well as specific ones (e.g. creativity, innovation, diplomacy).

2) Limit the competencies to no more than 10 – 15, maximum 20.

3) Review your achievements / activities / actions / incidences from your past work, ideally from the past

3 - 5 years but also sometimes further back, with a view to the competencies. Identify suitable examples which have a story to them reflecting your input and on which you would be able to speak engagingly for about 2 - 5 minutes. Exceptionally, examples can also be from voluntary and/or non-professional work or activities.

4) For each of the competencies, list 3 - 5 examples. Examples can be repeated for the various competencies. Attach a few key words / ideas to each example. For repeating examples, refer back to the first, more detailed citation under a main competency heading.

5) Now prepare an executive table with a maximum of 10 - 12 of the most important competencies for a typical job in your core or desired area(s). This should ideally fit onto one page, landscape mode. Exceptionally, it could cover more pages. Sometimes, competencies in job descriptions may contain sub-areas, emphasized by priority for the position (e.g. for "Professionalism": 1) data to results, 2) negotiations, 3) planning; for "Accountability": 1) time pressure, 2) rules, 3) shortcomings). In this case, you can mark examples according to the numbering of the sub-areas, e.g. "XYZ Sourcing Project 3".

If you wish or are under time pressure, skip step 4 and go directly to step 5 and the executive table.

Here is an example of an executive Table of Competencies:

1. Professionalism	2. Judgement/ Decision Making	3. Planning/ Organizing	4. Innovation	5. Communication
❖ Stakeholder Conference Dilemma to proceed in view of participant protest; conciliation meeting, sharing and co-development of agenda with stakeholders. ❖ Conference Stand Planning, coordinating with HQ and Regional Office under tight timeline; communication materials debate due to new corporate branding and gender balance issue. Success factors: identifying interests; pragmatism; team work.	❖ Emergency deployment of first aid kits Major logistics operation to dispatch emergency kits to island state A. Incomplete import documentation, engagement of Country Office in culturally sensitive item selection and facilitating customs clearance.	❖ Air Bridge Humanitarian crisis at X; despite lack of resources, successful establishment of 10 week air bridge with a consortium of logistics and humanitarian partners (UN, IFRC/ICRC, NGOs) in coordinated effort, saving lives. ❖ Conference Stand See 1. Professionalism	❖ Hybrid vehicle lease Lengthy approval process by technical department, pro-active clarification of details; result: cost reduction, emission reduction. ❖ New satellite-based online educational tool Needs determination with Field Office, settlement. After competitive dialogue process with entrepreneurs, public-private partnership with B, internal approval, testing, successful rollout, monitoring, end-user/feedback.	❖ Conference Stand See 1. Professionalism
6. Leadership	**7. Teamwork**	**8. Gender Equality**	**8. Diplomacy**	**9. Cultural Sensitivity**
❖ Batteries Dilemma to proceed with procurement for Y in view of urgent need, but missing local authorization/registration. Coordinated exemption together with Country Office.	❖ Conference Stand See 1. Professionalism ❖ Teamwork approach Challenge by Team Member on level of knowledge sharing within Team: Comprehensive vs. need-to-know basis. Trust, efficacy. Group discussion, SOP, follow-up.	❖ Conference Stand See 1. Professionalism ❖ Promotion in leadership position Appointment of Z as acting head of section during leave of incumbent. Active support, coaching; training in recruitment processes for career development.	❖ Batteries See 6. Leadership ❖ Legislation on environmental compatibility In country C. Shuttle diplomacy, meetings with all interest groups and stakeholders. Technical support in developing draft legislation; success by ensuring parliamentary-driven process.	❖ Emergency deployment of first aid kits See 2. Judgement/Dec. Making ❖ Basic necessities Case of critical press reports on basic necessities delivery; new planning and selection in country-led process in coordination with local communities and leaders.

Table 7 Table of Competencies with examples

6) For each of the examples you have selected for the executive table, write up a summary with key words on an A5-sized sheet. The summary, which you should be able to present in 2 - 3 minutes (maximum 5 minutes) during the interview, can be structured as follows according to the known STAR+L method (Situation, Task, Action, Result, + Lessons Learned):

- Headline reflecting in a nutshell what the example is about and why it is illustrative for the competency.
- Brief background, for understanding.
- Challenges involved in the case, constraints.
- Solution executed or supported by yourself. Be clear on your contribution.
- Any lessons learned, what you would do differently the next time.
- Enter any additional interesting aspects in bubbles in the right hand margin, on which you could expand if necessary during the interview or if you have a sure sense that you have more time, i.e. more than 2 - 3 minutes.

You may need to go through several iterations until you have transposed your real-life examples into clear, crisp, understandable and digestible bites. We tend to be longish on examples from our life, but with a bit of practice, these can be compacted. You may even undergo a cathartic sense of spiritual transformation in the process of recounting your experience. The result will also be much more appealing for your listeners. See an outline of an example on the next page.

To be practical, my recommendation is to work foremost with a basic set of 5 - 6 multi-use, fairly recent, major examples. These you can focus on in order to internalise them well and apply them for a larger range of competencies. E.g. a major project/challenge you have mastered in the past is likely to have covered all of analysis, judgement, communication, strategy, results-orientation and leadership competencies.

Practising speaking through the examples (as well as the "Why Applying" text, covered further ahead) and having half a dozen multi-use major examples at the ready is also critical for interviews in which consultation of notes is not permitted, i.e. the interview is conducted entirely in free speech / direct dialogue.

****

Satellite transmission project

Dilemma in innovation

A project on satellite transmission had to be completed against a tight timeline due to risk of donor withdrawal. A long-standing conflict among project players on an innovative aspect prevented conclusion.

After analysing the situation, I determined there were three issues to be resolved: A, B and C.

These issues I addressed by analysing the project agreement and the budget, and suggesting a small but significant change in priorities in respective activities and budget lines, related to implementation of the novel technical transmission standard. The small, but effective change was within the competency of the project manager and did not require going through the lengthy, formal project amendment process, to be endorsed in writing by all project partners.

[Possibility to expand on the specifics of the change and how it was possible to identify it.]

I held bilateral talks with the respective activity owners, followed by an online meeting among relevant players.

Result: success, the project could be concluded in time. Acknowledged by stakeholders and in the media.

Lessons learned: Due diligence and dialogue; use of project milestone tracking; ensuring inclusion of our Unit in project monitoring.

Table 8 Competency example narrative outline

_____ CHAPTER 7 _____

Written tests

You're invited to a test ? Awesome, you're one third of the way there to a new job !

Now you need to prepare for the test, and there are a few aspects to that.

First, some logistics. Where/when will you be sitting the test ? Are you able to choose a time within a certain given timeframe ? I would really try to avoid writing a test during work time, as it is cumbersome to arrange and you may be distracted, both through external events and internal reflections about your work/tasks. If there is no other way, it may in some cases be possible to request a change in time with the organisation/examining body, referring to your work constraints. However, before resorting to this last option, consider requesting leave of absence (half day) or leave for a personal affair if allowable, which are usually granted. Making clear that you will still be able to complete your work, attend to important matters etc. can be helpful. Some organizations will officially grant time for applications, but this could also lead to unwanted discussions /

perceptions / scepticism from colleagues, which can follow you for disproportionately long times.

Ideally you should sit the test at home, set up optimally for writing the test. If you can choose a time slot for the test, a clear choice is weekends or otherwise evening or early morning hours, depending on what type of person you are. I have sat tests at 6.00 AM in the morning, or at lunch times if there was no other possibility. If your place is far from work, consider renting a hotel room / office / conference facility nearby. It really may be worth the investment, and will help you concentrate. It may just lead to getting those extra points that will land you the job, a huge return on investment on the cost of the rented room/office, for years to come !

Ensure you have a secure, stable internet connection for the test. Is your browser technically compatible ? Have you performed all updates for the browser and the computer's operating system ? Do you have a backup PC/laptop and a reserve internet connection, e.g. your neighbour's Wifi or mobile data subscription ? Is your printer functioning, and is the printer cartridge well filled ? Is your printer installed in the PC/laptop you are using, with any necessary update ?

Now, on substantively preparing for the test. Here's a to-do list, to complete in the days / weeks before the test:

➢ Read the Terms of Reference / Job Description / Vacancy Notice line by line, and word by word. Are there any terms, abbreviations you need to look up ? What are the technical/functional areas ?

➤ Collect and review all relevant materials for the position. Both general background information about the organisation/department and specific material for the function. Index (number) the material as necessary, particularly allowing quick access during the test (that is if material is allowed). The information should be available at the tip of your fingers, otherwise it is essentially useless ! For some positions, there may be dozens of documents, e.g. relevant resolutions, policies, regulations/rules, manuals, strategies, papers, reports. Mark important parts with post-its, labelling these respectively, and highlight texts accordingly in the documents, adding any personal comments.

➤ Look at similar test questions/answers, e.g. from your past tests and official guidance documents.

➤ Note as indicated above that some test formats entirely disallow accessing any external material, and this is monitored by technical means and/or realtime web camera surveillance as communicated and agreed in the test conditions and following installation of respective software. That type of test modality may seem restrictive, however the good aspect is that all candidates are subject to the same constraint. You are therefore still competing on a level playing field and can show your skills and competencies and will be rewarded for these as in other test settings.

➤ In preparing for the test and also the interview, doing well is very good and laudable. But, you may attempt to take this a step further, maximising the success that you can achieve. Try to immerse yourself entirely into that new position, imagining already working in the position, with a view and drive from the inside. That may just give you the additional edge which will set you apart from competitors and ignite the spark with the assessor(s).

➤ Practice the test, simulating the test environment. Use sample questions, and/or make up your own questions or have a friend come up with some. It is important to get into the flow and the test situation before the actual test. These mock tests - they don't have to be as long as the real one, even a half hour or 20 minute practice session will warm you up - can work miracles for the real thing.

➤ Pay attention to time zones and that you will be ready on the set day at the required time. Summer time (daylight savings time) or similar time adjustments may move the effectual time forward or backward an hour. If in doubt, consult the world clock at http://www.timeanddate.com/worldclock/ and check the specific duration of summer times. For tests early in the morning, set two alarm clocks.

➤ As you get closer to the test, you might sometimes sense a negative attitude to the job or organisation, or general despair "woe is me". Pay attention to these feelings.

In the first case, is your subconsciousness in fact rejecting the perspective ? Will you be using the test to in fact, by way of underperforming, say "no" to the job opportunity ? If the answer to this question is in the affirmative, then do not sit the test, withdraw ! Or much better, change your attitude, and re-confirm this with yourself. Perhaps the new opportunity is not so bad ? If you are unsure about the opportunity, my recommendation would then be to sit the test in a positive spirit, viewing it as a challenge exercise, which will broaden your options and be giving you the time and space to reflect on your further path.

In the second case of feeling general despair, do not worry, this is normal. Acknowledge, recognise and allow for the feeling. Assure yourself that you will deal with this and, if you truly find there are issues to address, make a note of this in your rolling to-do list. However, for the time being the focus should be on the test.

➤ Before the test begins and insofar as permitted – see above - make sure you have all the relevant materials spread out at your location and within easy reach. Open up relevant internet sites and file folders / documents in your computer, if permitted. Close all sites and applications that you don't need.

➤ A few minutes before the scheduled time, take a moment of rest, close your eyes, breathe deeply, and then await the email / time to access the test link.

Tests can be multiple choice, written texts (essays etc.), case studies, simulations or a combination of these[7].

---

[7] See e.g. https://epso.europa.eu/en/selection-procedure/epso-tests; https://careers.un.org/lbw/home.aspx?viewtype=AP#Assessment exercise and Noreen O'Gallagher in Amrom, Dasha, *What does it*

The tests may be online or to be returned by email attachment. For online tests, sometimes it may not be possible to go back to previous questions/answers, which means that pacing yourself among the questions becomes very important.

Multiple Choice tests

For Multiple Choice (MC) tests, it's about arriving at the optimal balance among speed, focus and continuity. Going too slow or too fast can be equally detrimental. As Muhammad Ali put it, "*Float like a butterfly, sting like a bee*".

Read the instructions for the MC test carefully. Divide your time by question. E.g. for 25 questions in 50 minutes you obviously have two minutes per question.

Once logged into the test and the clock has started running, read any (further) instructions carefully and divide your time, if this could not be done in the earlier step.

Think quickly, but carefully about the question and the possible answers. As in "Who Wants to Be a Millionaire ?" and many similar quizzes/tests, there could be 1 – 2 outlier answers, and 1 – 2 more relevant, serious ones for each

---

take to land a job with the United Nations? (2014) on the website *Career Coaching Ventures (/Blog).* Link is omitted here, as the connection is flagged technically by the browser at the time of finalisation of this publication. However, the article and website are readily directly accessible via e.g. Google search (website access remaining at own risk).

question. Aside from directly identifying the right answer, a process of elimination can be helpful. Which answer(s) are less likely to be correct ? For some complex questions, this may be the fastest and sometimes only reasonable way to arrive at the correct answer(s) in the limited time. Taking a (very) long time is usually indicative of needing to reconsider the approach taken.

Note down any interim conclusions, calculations, results or commonly used data. For multiple e.g. parties/entities referred to in a question, a hand sketch of the respective relationships will help.

Generally try to avoid becoming too philosophical, e.g. seeking in very fundamental determination, if/when some-thing is *r e a l l y* true or false. Over-questioning matters ("smart*#&+") in most absolutist terms or existentialist way will regularly go too far. For example, a white flag is indeed white (true) and not non-white (false) due to impurities present on a nano-level in the fabric or its coloring. Remain reasonable and view the answer in relation to the other possible answers – together they constitute a finite (closed) set of answers.

On the other end of matters, there could be almost identical answers, though with some ever so slight, but essential difference – be vigilant and recognise such.

Particularly for questions in more qualitative fields requiring broader reflection, answers could accordingly differ by the greater or lesser degree of appropriateness or relevance as opposed to being entirely distinct from each other. It can also not be excluded on principle that a *multiple answer* format instead of multiple choice, i.e. where multiple answers are in fact allowed and rated (as in surveys, human resources assessments)[8], could be foreseen or introduced as well.

Once you have selected an answer(s), pause for a moment for affirmation. If possible, do a plausibility check on the answer. Particularly for mathematics/logic questions, try to validate your answer by common sense. When you have re-assured yourself of your selection(s), move on to the next question.

Always check how you are doing time-wise. If you are stuck and markedly over your time limit per question, move on to the next. If you are technically able to go back, you can revert to the question later, otherwise guessing will be the only choice (unless there is a point deduction for wrong answers, in which case a calculated risk will be necessary). Flag your unanswered or unsure questions with the e-marking facility usually available in the test application, or note them on paper and strike them off as you finish them.

Test formats and methods are subject to change as a result of experience gathered by the examining bodies and adaptation to requirements of operations. As an examinee, the best will always be to remain open and agile, adapting to the (new) circumstances, while mastering the skills that will always be needed: preparation, concentration and focus,

---

[8] See e.g.
https://docs.moodle.org/2x/pl/Multiple_Choice_question_type,
https://mettl.com/en/test/hr-competencies-assessment-test/.

association and expressiveness, agility and speed, dedication and determinedness, logic and common sense.

Written tests (Essays, memoranda etc.)

Further on preparing for the test in the days/weeks before the scheduled date:

➢ Make notes on the knowledge area / relevant examples from your work with respect to the position. Write up key words, key ideas, make lists or flowcharts. These should be complete, but at the same time not too lengthy/wordy, so that they will actually help you during the test and you can build on them (if consulting notes is allowed), and not possibly work to the contrary. On the next page for instance is a sample list of elements of a purchase contract, useful for legal or legal affairs-related positions.

➢ Some propose to write text modules of main or common issues in the relevant area, for copying into an actual text. However, this is not recommended, as it will in doubt be disallowed, and also, importantly, risks not being fit for purpose. The length will not be tailored to the actual needs of the test, i.e. either being too short or too long, and similarly the contents will likely require a different angle or focus, and this would therefore also be recognisable to the examiner(s).

When the test arrives, read through the instructions carefully, read the first question and print out the test

---

Contract Elements

Title

Preamble: Parties, "Whereas" clauses

Introduction: Definitions, background

Operational Part: Price, delivery terms, import/export licenses, payment, invoicing, warranty, liability, damages, indemnification, insurance, reporting, public relations, term/termination, ethics

Boilerplate clauses: Force majeure, confidentiality, dispute settlement, substantive law, exemptions (e.g. privileges & immunities)

Close: Signatures, names/titles, annexes

Table 9 Sample notes: List of elements of a purchase contract

simultaneously (if permitted). Now skim through the test in its entirety to get an idea of its scope. When you have ideas while reading/skimming through the text, jot these down immediately, as they come to mind. Reading through the entire test will start a background process where both your subconscious and conscious mind will begin to work on all questions while you are addressing a specific one.

Divide the time available, by question. Further divide the time per question into conceptualising and typing. Usually it's better to spend no more than 1/3 of the time available for conceptualising, better a little less, i.e. 25 – 30 %. Otherwise you risk not being able to enter all your good ideas into the machine. Some ideas will also pop up as you write. Stick to your planning as much as possible, you must really try to be disciplined in this. Time will usually be short, no matter how good your planning and how strong-willed you are.

E.g. for a 50 minute question, spend no more than about 15 minutes on the concept, and then 35 minutes on typing. Exceptions are possible, but should be used very sparingly, as there is high risk associated with this.

By the way, how fast can you type ? That is, words/characters per minute ? Test yourself e.g. at http://typing-speed-test.aoeu.eu/ . You should be able to reach at least 200 – 300 characters per minute. If not, consider an online typing class, or a 2 - 3 week classroom instruction. It can really be worth it to be able to touch-type without looking at the keyboard. And do you have a good keyboard ? Otherwise invest in one that has a good keystroke feeling and confirmation.

After you have divided your time, dive into your first question. It does not necessarily have to be the first question in the test, check if any order is possible. Some questions could, nevertheless, be built content-wise on preceding ones. Consider also that the answer to the first question in the test should ideally not be too weak, as first impressions count and otherwise the examiner(s) could inadvertently then be prejudiced in marking the rest of the test. On the other hand, there could be several examiners for different questions – you never know.

If you get hung up on a question, i.e. get writer's block, for more than just 1 - 2 minutes, move on within the question, or to another question, if possible, and plan for reverting later.

In your conceptualisation, sketch out all your ideas, basically performing a brain dump. Associate ideas freely, let your mind flow. Rarely is an idea too far-fetched not to note it down – you will be surprised about your own ability, and also how one thought may lead to the next. If you know where to find some information, pull in the relevant documents that you have pre-prepared and laid out at your location, if permitted. Consult the internet for information/ideas too, if allowed, and remember to quote any passages clearly in your answers (this would be expected to be prescribed in the tests if references are allowed; anti-plagiarism software may be applied to the tests by the examining body). Sometimes however, as mentioned, only originally written text of the examinee is permitted and outside source consultation is not possible. If you get stuck, look again at your initial notes, reread the question and briefly review prepared material again, if permitted, – any associations ?

Be careful not to be "top heavy" in answering a question, i.e. addressing a first part in detail, and the rest only scantily. This is a very common error, and it really takes practice to avoid. The same goes for the test as such: be sure to answer all questions equally / to the same extent in the test, and not just some or emphasizing a few and going light on the rest.

<u>It is much better to do moderately well on all questions than spectacularly on some questions and underperform or fail on the others</u>. Be conscious also not to waste time re-writing (typing) answers from other, foregoing questions if not necessary. You can copy-paste excerpts from other questions (if not disallowed), or also refer to these in such case without quoting text verbatim ("as elaborated in question 2, …").

> *It is much better to do moderately well on all questions than spectacularly on some questions and underperform or fail on the others*

If you ever really run out of time, as has happened to me on occasion, use the last 2 - 3 minutes to at least provide outline answers, i.e. bullets, comma-separated key ideas / issues, to the unanswered question(s). You will probably already have marked the ideas down in your notes or they will be on your mind. That may still earn you some valuable points for those questions and is in any case much better than instead leaving the test pages/entry fields blank, inevitably resulting in zero ratings for the questions.

Structure your answer. Use numbering, or at least paragraphs. This can be done in a few seconds, best before or while writing.

If you lack time during the test and it is not disallowed, as indicated above make ample use of time-saving bullets, hyphen lists, tables, comma-separated ideas, and refer to other parts of the test.

However you may feel during the test, do not despair ! Keep going, keep moving, remind yourself of your original flow and motivation and allow for re-establishing such. As mentioned, while you write, ideas may come up too. It's normal to undergo a sense of despair about 20 – 30 minutes into a 2 hour test. Yet one may very often be surprised afterwards as to what one was able to produce, even if at the outset one might have thought to have no idea of what to write and had a feeling of knowing next to nothing or worse, being a fraudster. Again, this is absolutely normal and only an obstacle that is there to be overcome and will be overcome. Weeks later you will marvel at your masterpiece and what your personal and professional potential in fact is.

You may also experience a flow or "high" in the approximately last third of the test, like an athlete in the final rounds of a competition. This is a good sign, use it, relish it, go with it ! It may be determining for the whole process. If you don't experience this sensation, however, don't worry, steady application can equally lead to success, and in any case there is no way to force the exuberance.

Watch the time carefully ! Get your text and valuable ideas into the computer, and pay attention if your input is not automatically continuously recorded (saved) by the test application. This can be a quite challenging part of the test.

All rules have exceptions, and this applies also to persevering vs. giving up on a test. There may be very exceptional cases where you realise you clearly have no chance, or the investment is not worth it, e.g. when you are essentially sure of having already secured another job. I would, however, guess that only perhaps in 1 out of 20 tests there could be such a situation and that you should permit yourself to give up. If in doubt, continue, see it as a challenge !

If you do give up, on the other hand, send a kind note to the Organization that you have decided to withdraw from the recruitment process, e.g. due to a change in planning or another good explanation. And offer your apologies for having caused any possible inconvenience.

There is commonly also a word or character limit for each question. Reserve about 10 % of the time you have allocated for a particular question, but usually at least 5 – 10 minutes, for final adjustment of the text to meet that text limit. Caution: if you are writing in MS Word or other text processing software, which I would recommend as above for the Q&A input in case of internet outage, and when transferring the text into an online data field, be aware that the word count in Word may not 100 % correspond to the word count in the online form. Some further last minute adjustments / experimentation may therefore be needed.

Once I had to shorten a text from some 3000 characters to 1500 characters or so, as I hadn't paid exact attention to the instructions. There were only few minutes left before the online clock expired, and it led to nothing but a disaster. The diligently entered text got chopped up, nice ideas were scrambled, resulting altogether in a rubble field of fragmented text and words. I had no hopes of passing the test and indeed didn't. Well: another learning experience or reminder …

As emphasized above, be sure to dispatch your test on time, before the deadline ! Do not poker or practice your brinksmanship skills on this aspect, be disciplined ! Online systems may be merciless in this regard, and also late email submissions may not be accepted by an organisation. Be sure in the last minutes that your internet connection has remained and will remain functional and that your browser/email provider is still operational.

In the best case, late submitted tests might only be penalized by point deduction or there may be a grace period, but this should absolutely not be counted on. The stakes are too high. Nothing is worse than not getting your valuable input, developed with such dedication and effort, into the system in time for assessment, and thereby dashing all hopes for the position. It has actually happened to me once after a five hour test and was a very tough lesson learned, and the only solace was that the position happened to fortunately be cancelled later by the recruiting organisation. And, I had actually written what I thought was "good stuff", which I was then able to add to my collection of materials, be it now only as a resource in preparing for other tests.

When you have sent off your test, take a few minutes to cherish the moment ! Capture the feelings and connect with your inner self. You have made headways into creating an opportunity for yourself, entirely of your own making. What a great accomplishment, reward yourself for it appropriately !

Case studies

These may necessitate a little more thinking and explaining than the ordinary test questions covered above, requiring prose answers. For mathematical/logic/financial questions, have a good working calculator at hand, if allowed. And brush up your spreadsheet / Microsoft Excel skills as necessary ! At least refresh the basics of calculations, formulae and formatting.

Some case studies could require drafting of a communication or document, e.g. memorandum, note for the file, presentation or similar. It's likely there won't be enough time to first write a handwritten draft before typing it up. I would go for a compromise in this case: sketch out the structure and list the main ideas, points of the document, and then type it up.

As mentioned earlier, beware of the risk of a top heavy document. Do not spend too much time on introductions / background, get to the core of matters within a reasonably brief period/space, the sooner the better. Revert later to fill up the initial part more, as necessary, time hopefully permitting.

Especially for mathematical/logic/financial questions, be careful and take time to ensure you have understood the question properly and that your answer(s) are reasonable. As above, do a plausibility check where possible, throughout. There is no point in rushing through the exercise and getting it quite wrong. Fewer words, but the correct path and calculation will normally be more valuable. If, on the other hand, it is taking very long for you to come up with the answer(s), or these seem overly complex, you are as mentioned above probably on the wrong path and should reconsider, if at all possible and correctable, i.e. time permitting.

After the test

After the initial high after finishing the test, there may be a period too, after a few hours or days, in which you may feel down, realising (or sometimes imagining) that you have missed this point or that one, or got something wrong, and exasperation may set it. No big worry, that's normal too. Most of the time, it's mostly unjustified. After a further while the larger perspective will set in again with the sense that your output was not so bad after all, and that e.g. you did in fact address some of those additional topics, or they were dispensable anyway or unfitting.

Conversely, you may sense you did well on the test and actually now have a chance at that new job. This may in turn propel you forward, but at the same time make you apprehensive of what is to come. In this situation, reflect on your original plan in setting out on a new job, and what your motivation and rationale were, and connect with these again.

For test materials that stay with you and are permitted to, e.g. those provided to you as text files and not only displayed online (in particular MC questions), and any answers prepared by you in text processing software, sort and file these materials away conscientiously. And celebrate this moment too, as your achievement. You may need the materials again or they may be helpful for another test, or for an interview. Index your tests by date and subject matter, for easy access (overleaf).

****

Index to Tests in Procurement/Supply Chain
(by sequential #, month/year and subject)

20.   12/21   Procurement plan, sourcing

19.   10/21   Supply chain risks, best value for money, system agreements

18.   06/20   Emergencies, end use monitoring, ethics, Corporate Social Responsibility

17.   03/19   ...

Table 10 Sample index to tests written previously

_____ CHAPTER 8 _____

Interview

So you've been invited for an interview ? Great, enjoy and savour the moment ! That is a definite honour, you've come a long way, and a successful conclusion is on the horizon. Congratulate yourself !

After your moment of reflection, start immediately with the preparations.

Check the date and time: Are they technically possible ? Is it a Skype/MS Teams/Zoom/Webex or other conference software interview, a telephone interview, or in person (more rare now) ? The same as for the written test applies: Best is an interview held outside of working hours, at a location outside of your office. Rent a hotel room or business centre facility nearby if needed – you need full concentration. If necessary, take official leave from work, be it half a day. In the very worst, unavoidable case - to be reserved only for the most serious exceptional situations, and still not recommended -, enquire if the interview could be rescheduled to a suitable date/time.

Read the Terms of Reference / Job Description / Vacancy Notice exactly again. Are there any terms, concepts you need to revisit ? Are the technical/functional areas clear ? Does the description contain any hints about specific challenges in the job that need to be overcome, e.g. *"eliminate backlog in …"*. Now assemble all the materials you had collected for the written test again, and add any additional ones with your renewed insight.

Before proceeding further with your planning, check whether the interview will be a technical interview, a competency-based interview or a combination of the two. The invitation will normally be indicating this. Otherwise, prepare for a combination version. I would not really recommend enquiring with the examining body, as this may generate a sense of indebtedness on both sides and imperceptibly raise the bar for the interview, just as the above re-scheduling would.

For a (partial) competency-based interview: Identify the competencies listed in the Terms of Reference / Job Description / Vacancy Notice. Does your table of competency examples cover these ? If not, add the additional competencies to the table, and ensure you have examples for them. See in general if your list of examples by competency requires updating in light of any recent experience at your workplace.

For technical questions, these are harder to predict, and the preparation is therefore the same as for the written test.

Prepare the 1 – 2 questions you may be allowed to ask the panel at the end of the interview. These questions should show your interest, while not making panel members feel uncomfortable due to any sensitivity or difficulty level of the questions. The questions should also not cover something that is already addressed in the Terms of Reference or on the website. For example, you can ask for details or examples on interactions with other relevant units, or on joint planning. The emphasis (share) of a new development / project / initiative in the overall work may be interesting too. The number of staff in a unit or subordinates and/or their category/level would be straightforward questions. If not clear, you can also ask if it is a new position or the vacancy is to replace the previous holder of the position.

Check that your PC/laptop is functioning, and that Skype/MS Teams/Zoom etc. are operating correctly. Has the latest update for the conference software been executed ? If (still) a phone interview, purchase an extension cable for your landline phone to reach your desk if necessary. Landlines are preferable to mobile phones, also due to possibly sensed emissions/e-smog during prolonged use, as in a one hour interview – arranging for one will be worth it.

Consider purchasing and using an external camera, e.g. one that you can position above your computer screen or slightly to the side of it, ideally being at eye level. An adjustable, angled stand for a notebook/laptop is a good alternative too and in any case a good investment for as little as 5 – 10 US$.

Why Applying:

Typically, a first question in the interview could be why you are applying for the position, i.e. your motivation, and/or what skills or value you are bringing with you to the job. For this part, prepare a one page narrative, which you can present in about 3 – 5 minutes. It should be clear and simple, pointing to main and decisive aspects. I would suggest to structure the text as follows:

- Personal Background: key qualifications, experience
- Main relevant skills / Competencies
- Specific aspects of the post that you find interesting <u>and</u>
- Your potential contribution in achieving objectives of the position in that regard
- Any further relevant elaboration on experience, activities, skills
- Main personal qualities / strengths
- Any personal aspects / links to the position, e.g. prior interaction with or visit to the Organisation / Department, alignment with its objective, approach.

This one-pager should be handwritten. This format helps to focus thoughts, be in touch with yourself and thereby to imprint the contents in your brain, for easy and smooth replication during the interview. Practice presenting this overview verbally a few times. See the example overleaf.

Why Applying

With the establishment of the new centre at XYZ I think this is a great opportunity to be able to apply the considerable expertise and skills I have gained in food and nutrition. I relish the challenge of getting the right balance between policy and practice. I am passionate about nutrition and new developments in it, e.g. on micronutrients. I am also interested in advisory and training aspects, in which I am equally experienced.

I have e.g. lately led a major study on seeds regulations and led training workshops on these. Generally with my more than 20 years of experience in food and nutrition I think I could add value to this position, specifically in relation to staple foods and ….

I am well familiar with the food and nutrition strategy of XYZ. I am fascinated also about the social aspects (e.g. links to poverty) and sustainability commitments. This is where I find my experience on seeds policy, oriented on the Sustainable Development Goals, is most relevant. …

I am an industrious, results-oriented professional, I pursue innovation and process optimisation, but am also a good listener and aim to build consensus. I think I could well bring these qualities to bear in this position at XYZ.

When I visited the office in (location) last year, I had the opportunity to interact with some of the Team. I would really look forward to working with the colleagues to achieve the goals lying ahead. I also fully identify with the evidence-based and holistic approaches of the organisation as well its innovation initiatives (in …) and sustainability objectives.

Table 11 Sample narrative of Why Applying

<u>Before the interview:</u>

A few days – at least 2 – 3 days - before the interview, start practicing answering questions before a partner / friend or just to yourself. Plan for at least 2 – 3 trials. The questions can be general (e.g. "*Give us an example where you demonstrated leadership skills. What were the important aspects, and were there any lessons to be learned ?*"). The questions as such are not so critical, what is important is – no matter how many interviews you have done before ! – getting into the flow, and into "interview mode". Also include the likely introductory and closing questions ("*Why are you applying ?*"; "*Do you have any questions for the Panel ?*").

If the position requires / desires additional language skills, brush them up ! If the additional language is only a complementary aspect of the post as opposed to a main/daily requirement, expect a question perhaps on a side aspect or "softer" competency, such as on staff induction, cultural diversity awareness. Prepare some 2 – 3 examples in that language for those questions.

Also, as an aside, if you need to visit the hairdresser, do so a few days before the interview, better than at the last moment. Similarly, hair wash a few hours before the interview may not be the best timing, though this is individual - whatever works for you.

I know, those trials of speaking through "Why Applying" and sample technical/competency questions can be a real put-off and source of procrastination before the interview. But believe me, overcoming that inner beast/chicken is worth every minute of it ! You will definitely feel much better and more confident for the interview. Also, don't be discouraged if some way into a trial, you experience a blockage, a type of "speaker's block", and you have the feeling you're not up to it and have to abort the trial. That's ok, easy on yourself ! It's normal, and you can relieve yourself by either verbalizing your feelings, taking a few deep breaths, and/or indeed starting over again. The sensation will fade away in the next trials.

A main point of the trials is, as mentioned above, getting into the flow before the interview. This is a necessary step for any person, and it is valid to say that practicing the presentation (Why Applying) / the contents of answers is secondary to that main goal.

Your last trial should not be too close to the interview, in order to give you some breathing and reflection space. I would suggest no less than 2 – 3 hours before the interview.

Start of the interview:

For interviews by video/audio conference or phone, dress and attend to personal care as you would for an interview in person. And dressing includes shoes, also for audio interviews ! Your voice and expression will reflect the rest of your body. For a video call, aside from being dressed properly (consider that you may need to get up unexpectedly during the call), make sure your place is well arranged, there are some colors and there is an overall pleasant scenery (try to apply some Feng Shui principles or other interior decoration recommendations). You can also use automated background settings in the conference application, e.g. blurring of background, light-coloured backgrounds. But do try out those technical functionalities prior to the interview. Check the lighting on your person, and how it looks on camera. Window blinds may need to be shut to eliminate glare. Improvision with paper sheets / cloth clipped before a lamp to create indirect lighting may also be workable. How are you positioned in the camera view ?

If it's not clear whether the interview will be audio or video, ask the organisation. Otherwise and/or according to the principle of not needlessly enquiring with the organisation and thereby also becoming indebted to it, prepare for a video interview since as mentioned you should dress accordingly anyway, presenting or radiating your best self.

Lay out all papers, materials and notes within easy reach on or around the desk that you will be sitting at for the interview, if allowed. Have your main papers (Table of Competency examples, technical materials, Why Applying, Terms of Reference of the position) and blank sheets of paper (better than a notepad requiring tearing off papers) close to you, as well as 2 – 3 pens/pencils. A glass of water may be nice too, be it for comfort, as usually there will be little time to quench your thirst or your sense of it. Lock and/or place a sign on the door if there is the risk of disturbance.

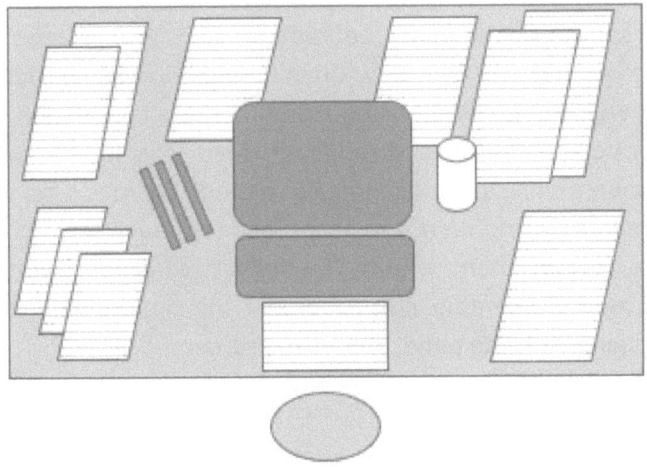

Figure 1 Arranging papers and equipment for the interview

Be sure to be ready on time for the interview. Time can fly just before such an event. A few minutes before the scheduled time, shut off any communication devices (not any phones including back-ups required for the interview) or other potential sources of disturbance and stand or sit at your desk, re-confirming that everything is in order. Take a deep breath, and gaze into the distance if you like, collecting yourself.

When the call arrives or connection is established, be courteous and return greetings nicely, be friendly, smile. As for the whole interview, whether audio or video, use facial expressions, body language, in any case make use of your hands. It is much more expressive. As indicated above, in audio calls, body language also affects what is transmitted to and sensed by the panel, i.e. radiates to it. In this sense, try always to take an overall positive demeanour, being friendly and welcoming, whether by audio or video connection. Let your personality shine through. In video calls, look at panel members while listening / talking to them. Try to engage with all members and do not focus or lean too much toward one or a few of them whom you maybe consider favorably disposed. Remember also to look at the camera lens when engaging with the panel, not at the screen !

During the interview:

In general, the interview requires a balance between preparation and spontaneity. Preparation is essential, but is always secondary to the actual situation. The prime objective is to listen intently to the specific question(s) being asked and to give best resonating responses. As you listen to the question, what comes to mind ? Jot down your thoughts on paper as they come. Use arrows, key words, abbreviations, underlinings – whatever helps and you are accustomed to. I find that taking notes generally helps with the association process and frees up your mind for additional thoughts. It looks professional too.

For a competency question, do you have a decent, pinpointed example to present in response to the question ? If so, go with it, also if this was not among the examples you had prepared. If not and if in doubt, and with no other more relevant example coming to mind in the meantime, take a prepared example from your Table of Competencies.

Track the time in answering. If you know beforehand how many questions there are, the average time available is clear. Avoid being too long, and get to the main point(s), i.e. your actions and achievements, fairly rapidly. Be concise, but at the same time do not appear overly short, i.e. brisk. If the panel must drag the answers out of you, or has to become inventive to fill the time or a sense of silence that has come up, this will usually not be so favourable. A presentation of 3 – 5 minutes should regularly be suitable and leave room for any follow up questions.

If you think two smaller examples would be more suitable than one regular example – ask the panel at the outset before answering or indicate this is what you like to do.

For technical questions, a bit more initial reflection time may be useful before answering. Not only content, but also structure and thought process, line of argumentation may be rated. You can take this time, while e.g. noting key ideas and sketching out a line of thought. Use arrows and figures/symbols if helpful. Should a question remain unclear in any respect, ask for it to be repeated or reiterate it yourself the way you understood it.

If you find you are on the wrong track with your example or solution – and it is not just a case of "speaker's block", requiring a moment to gather composure, ask for permission to re-start with a more appropriate example or better fitting solution if you have such in mind. This may be granted. If not, don't worry too much either - your perception may well be for the most part subjective -, and instead proceed to highlight the particularly relevant aspects of the original example or solution, perhaps even things or aspects you had not thought of beforehand during your preparations / brainstorming.

Otherwise and in general, go with the flow and dynamics of the interview. Do not let yourself be distracted by any noises, other occurrences, or also a (perceived) setback such as the above or other (perceived) discouragement. For audio communications, focus on the voices of the panel members.

Try again to do fairly well in all questions rather than brilliantly on a few and poorly in others. Do not let your guard or concentration down on any particular question, including any seemingly "easy" question. Always do your best, and associate ideas the best you can.

> *Try to do fairly well in all questions*
> *rather than brilliantly on a few*
> *and poorly in others*

In no event let yourself be tempted during the interview to display any sense of desperation in getting the job, or doubts about your performance, even if your inner feelings may be diametrically opposed to such and you would rather wish to do nothing but precisely such, conveying the despair both in regard to the possible job and maybe the general state of affairs. It will be of consolation in this regard that the panel will not be interested in how horrible you may find your current job, or how your job, family or other commitment made it difficult for you to prepare for the interview, or any other challenge(s) that you may be facing. The panel overridingly only wants to see the best of you and how this matches the organisation's needs. And so this, on the flip side of matters, should and will make it easier for you.

And if, on the other hand, before or during the interview you sense you are at an advantage to obtain the position, believing to perceive such during the interview or having been given to understand such beforehand by someone, never assume this is indeed the case and/or that the interview is indeed or will be a shoe-in. Give the interview all you have, apply yourself fully as for an entirely regular interview. An interview thought to be a sure bet can be most treacherous.

End of the interview:

Keeping up your chin also applies to the closing of the interview. If invited, ask the 1 – 2 questions you have to the panel. At the very end, be courteous and respectful; do not let yourself be tempted into any casual / nonchalant final remarks or exclamations. That can subconsciously, and depending on circumstances, be interpreted negatively and cast a veil onto the foregoing, otherwise positive exchanges. Thank your counterparts courteously for the interview.

If you are invited to follow up on the interview with any additional questions, do so, be it out of courtesy and/or to demonstrate your interest.

If you have experienced any significant adverse circumstances during the interview (e.g. technical difficulties), you may mention this to the organisation. Though normally such circumstances should be brought up as and when they occur, i.e. during the interview, so that they could be addressed. Otherwise you may also be seen as having implicitly been agreeable to them.

After the interview

Generally, resist enquiring with the organisation about the status of your application. Continue with life as before. Only in exceptional cases, where you sense there may indeed e.g. be a mix up with the tests or some other irregularity, contact the organisation.

A longer period of silence usually means a rejection. However, rejections are part of the process, so don't worry - move on. While rejections need to be acknowledged and suffered through at that moment - with the pain usually unfortunately being directly proportional to the expectancy and hopes associated with the particular job -, they are just a momentary occurrence and experienced sensations will pass.

It may seem contradictory, but honour those "NOs", revere them with modesty. It's part of the game, you are learning and each one makes you more knowledgeable and stronger. If you are doing your best, you are on the right track and sooner or later you will be successful, and those "NOs" will fade away into the depths of eternity in the light of the one "YES" ... So don't worry and stay positive !

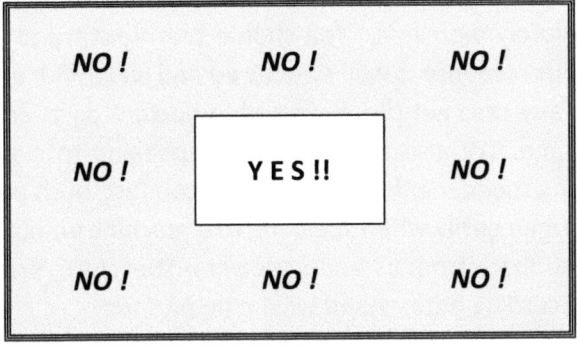

Figure 2 Getting those NOs and a YES

Automated interviews

Some people may find an automated/machine interview more challenging than an in-person interview. The human interaction and feedback are missing, and the process may feel lifeless. On the other hand, you may find you have more control of the situation.

In any case, the preparation is the same as for a live interview, and if it helps one can imagine speaking to personal counterparts. Even a printout from the company website with persons or representations placed in sight may be helpful.

It is important to listen to / read the individual question carefully, make notes, and in preparing and recording the response, be very conscious of the set time limit. The minutes/second counter visible on the screen counting down is absolutely merciless ! You should therefore try to ensure that your response is well structured and weighted, and that you in any case get the main and important parts across in good time. Try also to adjust your speaking to a regular, engaging speed, neither too slow nor too fast, both of which can happen easily when speaking to a machine without real-time feedback from listeners/viewers. Therefore, practicing such recording beforehand will be helpful too.

Pre- or post-pended Interviews

Sometimes a preliminary interview ("get to know interview") or final/secondary confirmatory or decisive (tie-breaker) interview may be held as well.

These interviews, at times appearing or made to appear light-footed or low impact, may just well be the very opposite, i.e. key/critical steps in the recruitment process under the guise of inconsequentialness. Therefore, beware, do not let yourself be bedazzled in any way, and take these interviews at least just as seriously as a regular, formal interview, i.e. with all relevant preparations and attention. I have witnessed such, with preliminary or confirmatory interviews in hindsight appearing by all means decisive.

For example, a "get to know interview" can turn out to be as intensive as a regular one and also to be suddenly the only and final one. Or, a regular interview could take place with all the relevant specialists and managers, basically fronted in the process, while the final "confirmatory" interview is a repeat together with the actual decision maker, who may then take an entirely different approach/view, be it just to show or remind his/her subordinates who is calling the shots or, worse, to undermine the choices of his/her staff and weaken these, for his/her short-term personal gain. From a process point of view, this approach would certainly neither be efficient in terms of use of resources, nor would it inspire confidence in the organisation or its leadership, however, regrettably, possibly sometimes a reality to deal with.

****

_____ CHAPTER 9 _____

Y E S !

The organisation has written back indicating it is pleased to inform you that it intends to offer you the job ? Bingo, you've made it, yes ! Congratulations, your steady dedication has paid off !

Write back promptly and kindly, confirming your continued interest and availability.

Choices:

You're thinking of taking another job instead, which you are hopeful of still getting ? Careful, this is a mine pit ! It is very easy to miscalculate this and gamble away both jobs, leaving you with NOTHING but your old job. Why did you go through the ordeal of the selection process, only to cast out the new opportunity at the end ? Unless you have been granted a reflection period of a few days and there is a chance of your other job actually materialising in that period, take the job that was offered to you. Do not bank on an other job for which you have no firm commitment.

Some job advertisements also indicate that the recruitment process carries expectation of accepting the job offer if selected, and there could therefore be consequences if this is not followed.

You're in the lucky position to really be able to choose between two or more job offers ? How do you do that without regrets ? There are several books on decision making covering that type of situation[9]. The best advice I can give is to imagine yourself in each of the new job(s) for a few hours / days. What is your state of being and what are your respective feelings ? What is your sense of regret in respect of the turned downed job(s) ? Where does the sense of fulfilment most outbalance the sense of regret ?

Transition:

The transition period to the new job can be smooth or quite rough and difficult. Doubts, apprehension and downright fear may arise. Not only your job situation, but your partnership, overall life situation, your earlier years, pretty much everything may suddenly appear in doubt and at disposal. You may no longer be thrilled, have low or no energy and no motivation, and just when you need these

---

[9] E.g. *The Decision Book: Fifty models for strategic thinking* by Krogerus, Mikael and Tschäppeler, Roman (2017), new edition, Profile Books.

most and least expect the opposite. Tip: Stick with your plan from 1 – 1 ½ years ago to get a new job, unwaveringly. Execute it, just do it. Do not start mixing issues and let yourself be steered off course. Instability, uncertainty ? Acknowledge these, but stand your ground, you will get over it, believe me.

Be easy on yourself. Use tools available to you such as taking remaining vacation (best to have built this up in advance), sick leave if you are feeling unwell, working only core hours and arranging your time flexibly around them, seeking out friends and family, resources, basically anything that will help reduce stress, anxiety and/or suffering. If you're very anxious, visit the new place if you can, be it just in order to be in the city / the neighbourhood (or use Google Maps). It's a natural instinct. Try to avoid looking back.

Psychology says there are four phases to change: Denial, Resistance, Exploration, Commitment ("Change Curve")[10]. I would in fact add a fifth one "Enthusiasm" at the outset, as this is what got the process started from your side in the first place. You will normally always go through all these phases, some people more intensely than others. Some get stuck in the stage of resistance/regret and want to return to the

---

[10] See e.g. Jaffe, Dennis and Scott, Cynthia, *Mastering the Change Curve* (2012), http://de.slideshare.net/cynthiascott/mastering-changecurveassessmentpaper. The Change Curve is based on the original work of Elisabeth Kübler-Ross, *On Death and Dying* (1969), see https://en.wikipedia.org/wiki/K%C3%BCbler-Ross_model. There is also the suggestion by David Kessler to add "Meaning" as a final stage, ibid.

status quo, their current job. You should resist this play of the senses and instead have your sights set clearly on the new, positive perspective and the opportunity it presents, also for personal development.

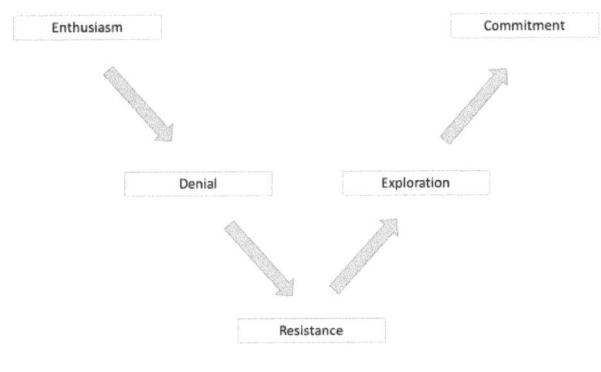

Figure 3 Change sequence

You're thinking indeed of staying on in your current job, perhaps suddenly realising or idealising its benefits, and/or suddenly becoming very attached to your current location/environment ? Or, suddenly that fire is reignited in you to persevere and (finally) make it at your old workplace, to rise further in the ranks, best to the upper echelons. Careful, as mentioned these are likely illusions, fallacies of the mind, and only very rarely are such considerations actually justified, i.e. should you stay with the status quo.

You have already embarked on your new path a long time ago when you decided to get that new job and sent off that application. Therefore let go, respect and honour your prior considerations and initiative.

Even if you are indeed enticed back to your old job with an improved work area, career level/progression, salary/ benefits or the outlook thereof, this can be a disappointment in reality over time, and your current employer may only have done so to cover your managers' (bad) conscience or ward off any potential impending criticism for having lost you. If after realising such manoeuvring and the idealisation of the old job, and any other sobering reality sets in, the almost certain sense of regret of having stayed on may become overwhelming over time, running you into a downright depressive state. Then, the sense of regret will outbalance any new ostensible benefits at the old workplace, as well as the benefits of having discarded the other opportunity, and there will be no way bar Star Trek time travel to return back to the original decision point.

Your spirit has desired change – give it the space and allow it to happen. Yes, you may feel uneasy for some 3 – 6 months. But it will get better and it will definitely be worth it in the mid and long run.

When it's time to terminate your old position, do so unhesitatingly. And yet, try to keep the public drawdown phase to a minimum at your old workplace, to limit potential uneasiness, pain or other difficulties. It could e.g. occur that individuals or the organisation as such might not receive the news of the departure favorably, dropping some snide comments, introducing bogus hurdles or even exercising vindictiveness. Also, routine tasks or processes might suddenly become encumbered. While this negativism is best met with stoicism diligently mastered over the years, it is still hence best to limit this unpredictable transition period.

At the new organisation, strike a positive-friendly tone in your further communications with your new counterparts, establishing a good basis. Avoid too many demands, special requests and haphazard queries. Many questions may just be posed out of curiosity, out of the desire to communicate with the new counterparts (about anything) and may in fact be answerable from publicly available sources or common sense. Where really necessary, try to rephrase questions into indirect/polite enquiries ("*I wanted to enquire whether it would be possible to receive further information on the medical coverage of dependents*") or confirmatory statements ("*I understand that ...*"). Interaction with thoughtless demands and questions may otherwise quickly turn sour, even if not explicitly expressed by counterparts, a circumstance which will be hard or impossible to correct again further on.

When leaving your old job, try to do so with grace, gratitude and compassion. For your closest associates, you may wish to let them know in advance. Give a farewell party if you are up to it or at least write a kind farewell message to all, expressing thanks for the time you were able to spend at that organisation and the opportunity of working with your colleagues (or any other positive message that you feel comfortable with). Bid farewell to professional counterparts at other organisations, clients etc. too, if you find this will be accepted by the present organisation or in fact welcomed in its corporate culture, taking the opportunity also to outline any new arrangements. Definitely avoid any negativities in your communications – you don't know when/where you will be interacting with colleagues and counterparts again, i.e. do not burn bridges. The farewells are also important on a personal level for achieving closure in the change process.

By the way, if instead of receiving a job offer you are placed on a roster, valid for a year or longer and extendable, that's certainly something to celebrate too. It's maybe already 50 % of the way, if not in some instances more or close to 100 %, to a new job ! It may now just be a matter of time, and sometimes active follow-up with counterparts could be helpful as well to spur things on. It's common to hear of cases where a candidate was initially put on a roster, and then after just two or three months is basically 'ordered' to his/her new post. Or after a half year of tranquillity, things suddenly move very fast, expediting medical and document checks, references, visa and other travel requirements, employing express courier services, i.e. the long sought job suddenly materialises very concretely and at high speed.

****

P A R T 2

_____ CHAPTER 10 _____

New job

Being at your new job means *New game, new fortune* ! Trust your experience and instincts. Having said that, be aware that every organisation and new job is different, in a different setting. Therefore be open. Perhaps the new situation requires a new evaluation and approach. Don't assume that things which have worked elsewhere will work here, or that e.g. the Communications Department is strong or weak, and that the Human Resources Department is helpful or unhelpful, and the Staff Association has a certain role or degree of influence.

My recommendation would be to observe and listen before acting, just go with it – and that period may take several weeks or months. Converse in interested manner with a wide range of colleagues, engage in dialogues. Both as a manager and "own operator", try to introduce changes that you think are necessary or advantageous only after you have understood the system, its unspoken rules, networks, inside pecking order, de facto management, culture, and what works and doesn't work. However, this is not a universal rule, and can be individual and dependent on the situation. Some fixes may need to be insisted on right at the beginning, otherwise they may realistically never be implementable.

Staying positive and kind, extending a degree of trust to people before being disappointed, while being healthily cautious about reports, statistics, data, etc. presented to you and particularly alleged "ways of doing things", customs, hearsay, gossip and rumours, should normally be a good compass to orientate yourself by. Aside from the unreliability of the information, be aware of underlying interests or motives there can be in presenting or mentioning things to you as a newcomer.

Be cautious about initial traps that can cause long-term harm or doom. There's always good reason to be optimistic, but who said the new job would be a piece of cake ? There may be attempts to foist downright hazardous or toxic cases onto you as you start up. They can be masked as harmless, minor actions left over by a predecessor etc. Entry to a job can then mean exit not long after. Therefore, approach these cases with the same diligence, circumspection and strategy that you would in your regular course of work (next chapter).

Or otherwise, you could also become compromised by such hazardous cases before you know it, becoming part of a network of questionable performance in return for seeming favourable on-looking, inclusion in part of a "gang" or other clique/mafia-type structure. But your initial bailout and sense of comfort come at a price. Payback may be expected in due course, and repeatedly, beyond any initial sacrifice/investment made. Worse, such trap could have been set deliberately, to create greater dependency.

In general, joining "gangs" is a risk-fraught and potentially hazardous undertaking, apart from in all likelihood being against institutional structures and policy. You will be associated with the gang or perceived as such, enveloped by its groupthink, and pay for the dealings of the gang in one form or another ("cling together, swing together"). And, will the gang come to your rescue when you are in need or trouble, or will you instead be left out high and dry ? If there is a 'rescue', what form will it take, and might it not in fact be getting you into even deeper trouble ? It is in any case a downwards spiral, potentially turning faster and deeper. Exiting from such groups will then not only be rather difficult, but may also be downright hazardous. In such instances, departure from the organisation may consequently perhaps be the only option left.

Further, when bound to a particular grouping, if one day you would wish to take a stand on an issue in the organisation, take an initiative, or speak your mind, you could find it next to impossible for fear of repercussion(s), even if that fear might mainly be subjective.

While staying clear of particular groupings may be difficult, this can in the long term - after restructurings/reorganisations, special audits and other 'raids' – prove to be just that essential job saver and step in advancing your career.

Best in my view is to maintain personal integrity, to stay ethical and true to yourself, resisting groupthink, retaining your possibility of free speech, freedom of opinion and expression within the context of the organisation, your reality and truth, and remaining – while well connected in the organisation – an own operator, i.e. unaligned, and accountable in first instance to yourself.

****

_____ CHAPTER 11 _____

On the job

Be positive at work. Engage with people: People of all kinds – senior leadership, managers, associates, assistants, your peers, drivers, security staff, cafeteria staff, couriers, regardless of your own position. Shed yourself of any prejudices you may hold. Respect and implement gender and other social policies. Have an open door policy.

At the same time, keep up with your work. Ensure to advance the major, big-ticket items alongside daily requirements and distractions. Address matters here and now, avoid deferring indefinitely and do not ignore matters of concern. If/when you defer matters, be sure to have a system for tracking them and regularly issuing reminders to yourself. Avoid creating or sustaining time bombs or skeletons. Do not allow those mine fields and closets to establish themselves, or clear them out as early as possible !

If you are awaiting input from others, track these responses too, send kind reminders in intervals. In a to-do list, you can put a circled P for "pending" in front of all actions points for which you are awaiting input/response from others.

Maintaining an email folder called "Awaiting response" or "Pending response" with copies of sent query mails, can also be useful, though such folder can also easily get cluttered or overflow with time.

Time management

Time management (prioritisation of work) may be the most important skill to acquire. It takes discipline and sometimes years of experience to implement this effectively. Avoid being trapped in the dozens of emails pouring in every day. One can be busy with emails all day, and still basically have accomplished next to nothing. Keep your focus on substantive, value-adding work and ensure to prioritise it. As mentioned, bring forward your big projects. Progress is the direct result of incremental steps and good time management. Set aside, if need be forcefully "carving out", the required time for such important tasks from your weekly time schedule.

Also use travel time and other "slack" to progress with those major undertakings. Those times can be best opportunities for being undisturbed and concentrated. Travel can therefore be a great catalyst for advancing matters. Just trade in the armchair in a lounge for a cubicle with a desk. Sometimes all that is needed is a short note to self on your phone, or paper and pen/pencil, to advance your big ticket items, and for that matter a napkin will also suffice for noting down main ideas at a coffee table, just do it !

Working as a team

Interacting with other team members and working as a team may be challenging through no fault of individual team members. The root cause may in my view lie not so much in individual characters or assignment of roles, but in the education or training the team members have undergone. Curricula seem to have been created with a view to developing the best expert, e.g. in communication, quality assurance, engineering, finance, law or other area. However, everything is interconnected, and while other, adjacent disciplines are most of the time usefully covered in these curricula to the extent needed in the primary discipline, there appears to be lastly little or in any case insufficient coordination with the curricula and approaches taught in these other fields. Arriving at mutually beneficial and compatible outcomes can then be significantly encumbered.

Now, in a team setting, all these best educated experts, a "team of stars"[11], are suddenly called on to collaborate, in achievement of a common goal. As these results are to be achieved in the real world, with very real timelines and constraints, difficulties - if not disaster – on both professional and personal levels are effectively pre-programmed. Worse also, without strong leadership coordinating the input, when it comes to output, a colourful but altogether incoherent

---

[11] See in this regard e.g. the article by Toegel, Ina, IMD (Institute for Management Development, Switzerland), *From a team of stars to a star team* of 17 May 2022 at https://iby.imd.org/human-resources/from-a-team-of-stars-to-a-star-team/.

potpourri of information, best practice and/or requirements, oftentimes also contradicting each other, may then be presented to the outside world.

Collaborators in a team are therefore called on to make compromises on their ideal output, sometimes quite considerably. That is, if anything significant is to be achieved before team members retire in maybe 20 or 30 years ! This pragmatic approach appears not to be taught or emphasized sufficiently in education.

What is most important in working as a team ? Communication: verbal, written, or with any other media. Ideas, knowledge, expectations and limitations need to be communicated and understood within the team. Active listening is the single and most effective component – and easy to do: just taking the time and patience to become aware of and understand what a team member is thinking, expressing and planning or expecting will go a long way in charting and proceeding along a common path.

Being respectful, understanding and cooperative, but at the same time clear on own capacities (substance, competencies, lead times), expectations and boundaries, is a good orientation point for both coming through and flourishing in a team. When team members practice transparency, sincerity and approachability, without becoming lost in micro details, pedantry, undue questions of ego and other petty squabbles, a strong fabric is crafted for successful team cooperation.

Exaggerations, exuberance and other office blossoms

"This report is a disaster", *"The data is wrong"*, *"We will be flooded with emails"*, *"So-and-so was really pissed off"*, *"This will have catastrophic consequences"* or *"This will cost us 10 mn US$"* are some examples of office hype and exuberance. It is better to not let oneself be absorbed by such and instead remain level-headed, applying common sense and verifying matters as necessary. Rarely are events and occurrences as absolute and consequential as recounted in these exaggerated ways. The report was perhaps only questionable in certain passages, only some of the data was incorrect, a colleague's alleged rage was perhaps directed at something close by, but distinct, and the cost estimation did not take into account economies of scale and parallel savings from redundant activities.

Similarly, *"So-and-so is taking too much leave"* could, for instance, be found after closer inspection to be untrue when examining overall statistics. Perhaps it is actually only the frequency of leave or the short notice period of applications for leave that have been found bothersome, and not the cumulative length ? Positive accomplishments may equally be presented in exaggerated manner, as in *"People were absolutely blown away by the presentation/figures"*. Applying objective standards, indicators, measurements and comparators will be helpful in these situations.

It's easy to get stuck on tasks or challenges because of being focussed on yes / no, accept / reject, go / no-go or other black-and-white options. E.g. *"I cannot provide the report by the end of the week*". Ok, but is it possible to provide an overview, an outline or perhaps a first draft ? Can the report be split and a colleague may be able to help ? Find a middle ground, propose a compromise, think in-between things and in gradations. This will avoid getting hung up and reduce frustration and arguments, and instead set things in motion.

> **Lisa is taking too much leave !**

Example of exaggerated or unfounded exclamation

Ensure that significant matters are done or confirmed in writing. At the same time, do not write carefree/careless emails/text messages, even to alleged "best friends". Only write emails/messages that can stand over time and that you would be able to defend if broadcast on TV, tweeted, blogged or otherwise made public. Emails and messages are read and/or can be retrieved, and might sometimes find their ways to unintended recipients. Yes, it is true that emails and messages can be retracted as opposed to documents, but one should not count on that technology always functioning and/or the retraction being executed in time, e.g. before quick readers have accessed them on their iPads, iPhones or other devices. Where appropriate, talking on the phone or in person could be an alternative.

Trust is a good human trait, but preferable is to remain circumspect and realistic. Some people speak differently, sometimes diametrically opposed, to different audiences. If you need to get clarity on someone's position, raising the issue in an open, common forum with several participants, including the concerned, and ideally with the relevant stakeholders present, is a possibility. Or, if in writing, copying relevant colleagues into the correspondence, may be effective. Even if it could feel awkward, it is worth it.

If volunteers are requested for an activity / position, do consider in earnest to propose yourself. It's an easy way to get involved and enrich your experience. Oftentimes the work/hours involved are much less than first considered. Sometimes no work at all is needed !

Do not bypass people. Even if you know their position will not be to your liking, give them a chance to respond, and send a reminder if they remain silent. Otherwise, the relationship may be damaged for some time or become beyond repair. Only after these steps have been exhausted, reach out a level higher, while still copying in the original addressee.

If something went wrong, there's sometimes the tendency to swing to another extreme to attempt to prevent the occurrence in future (in supply and logistics: "bullwhip effect"). Yet, on closer examination, the new "fix" may not even address the underlying error – e.g. human error, negligence/incompetence in applying an otherwise entirely satisfactory and functioning process, rule or regulation. The "fix" may thus instead be targeting unrelated situations / persons. The "fix" could even serve as a cover up for recognised underperformance. In a best case, the "fix" may only be strongly exaggerated, with little practical relevance, and only thereafter introduce slowness, complications and barriers into the process. Hence, if in your own realm, analyse the problem carefully and thoroughly, and only put forward truly applicable, necessary, proportionate and relevant responses for rectifying an issue. If within someone else's remit, comment where possible on respective propositions or other ostensible remedies.

If you have good ideas – and these will come – about your work, your strategy, your plans, your career etc., note them down ! Regardless of the time of day or where you happen to be – the ideas may never come again. If needed, note them in your mobile phone or send yourself a text message or, the old-fashioned way, tie a knot in a tissue.

Remain flexible in your work at all times. If you've made a mistake, correct it. We are all humans and mistakes happen, they are part of the process. Output and products are rarely perfect, and there's normally no such absoluteness as *"the report is finished"*, *"the email has been sent off*, *"I already told them no"* etc. Only very few events are set in stone, at least for a while. Therefore adjust, correct, add, also last minute or post-deadline, as needed. Send updated versions or comments after requested submission dates/times, or comment verbally. Rarely are these addenda flat out rejected, in fact they may oftentimes be appreciated, as frequently not many coworkers actually do send feedback, and often a first communication has not even been seen by others or its contents reviewed before receiving a second communication.

Asking questions only to demonstrate subordination to a superior or, all the worse, succumbing to pretending not to comprehend something or even to underperforming in order to demonstrate subordination, are damaging habits and therefore definitely to be avoided. Though, such behaviour can also happen subconsciously, be it ever so slightly, to the best intended staff. Certainly there is no need to ask unjustified or daffy questions, or to ask questions just for the sake of asking questions, in order to demonstrate loyalty or subordination. Respect for line managers etc. can rather be reflected well by listening attentively to them, ensuring understanding, executing tasks diligently, raising issues or enquiring in constructive way where indicated, being supportive, and where appropriate anticipating tasks, challenges.

Complexity

Avoid and reduce complexity wherever you can. Administrations and operations frequently suffer under the constant desire for more precision and information. It's then easy to get drowned by it. Information can also be misused to obscure or delay matters. Therefore, while information is principally a positive asset, as it regularly ensures more transparency and objectivity, it should only be generated and used where it adds actual value. It's important in this regard to always maintain the big picture and understand the basic significance of the information. What is trying to be explained or conveyed with the information ? What impact does it or can it have ? Will too much information achieve the opposite of the intended effect ?

For complex processes, documents, and if you are asked or wish to summarize, comment or elaborate on them, consider making some tables, charts, graphs etc. It really helps to visualize and understand complex issues at hand. Also, it makes it much more interesting for readers or the audience. You can also do this ad hoc at a meeting, drawing on a flip chart or on a pad of paper. If the result resonates with participants, take a picture of it with your phone and incorporate it into your commentary and/or distribute.

As a manager

If you are a manager / supervisor, trying to avoid setting rules that will come back to bite you, is good practice. E.g. it is very hard to establish when staff should copy you on emails and when not. On the one hand, understandably you may wish to reduce your daily workload, but on the other hand, for sure you would not want to be blamed for not knowing something because of your own restrictive rules on copying emails. It is in such situation preferable to instead ask staff to use their best judgement, that is what they are employed for in first instance in any case.

Similarly, avoid instructing or managing staff too closely (micromanagement). Not only would you probably be able to complete the work yourself during the instruction and follow up time, but importantly also your staff will likely lose motivation and let their boss do the work or wait until they get more detailed instruction and even maybe seek confirmation thereof before taking action. It's a bottomless pit, that can get you entangled and/or caught in a snare.

> ***Management Instruction:***
>
> ***"Do not CC XYZ on emails"***

Risk-fraught management intervention

If you are coordinating matters, a tool that can work wonders when exercising the necessary patience is the consensus-based approach. This involves buy-in or at least non-objection of the involved, in order for the group to find consensus. Importantly, in difficult instances the consensus process requires that persistent opponents of an action are then called on to explain what it would take to make the action work or to reach an objective. And, to avoid unproductive blockage, overwhelming majorities are also possible.

Every rule, however, has its exceptions, and that of course applies to the consensus-based approach too: sometimes (controversial) leadership and executive decisions will be called for to move ahead in timely and/or effective manner. Yet these should also thereupon be communicated in transparent way and discussed.

Open office space

Working in a common office space takes some time to adapt to. It's not sure how much more effective this organisational method really is. True, coworkers are sitting close by each other, but it can occur they might not really talk to each other for weeks or months (so close, but so far away, they could be on other sides of the equator …). The noise level and other emissions can be disturbing too. Some staff may therefore resort to earphones or earplugs and other distancing devices and techniques, such as folder stacks, plants, flags. Also to be watchful of undesired eavesdropping. For phone calls that prospectively take longer than about a minute, it is safer, better or also probably in keeping with office etiquette to take your wireless/mobile phone outside. For important/conference calls, these should be scheduled in advance and a meeting room booked with a conferencing facility, or the possibility to bring your own device.

New to a system ?

In large intergovernmental development organisations, such as the UN or EU, if coming to such from the private sector, government, smaller or medium-sized NGOs, or other institutions, the environment may be a culture shock, both at first and after some time again. People may consequently experience a personal crisis after 1 – 2 years, frustrated at the way of getting things done and apparent onerousness or slowness of the organisations. Respect for rules and procedures can indeed slow down operations, sometimes to a grinding halt for extended periods, though this need not be so and can depend on individual attitudes. At such point, staff which are new will face the choice: to stay, move on or move back ? Fight, flight or freeze ? It's a choice. If you do choose to stay, the tools described in this book will help you stay in the organisation and advance on your path. That I can assure.

Handle yourself with care. Moving to an entirely new surrounding is never easy and takes time. In gardening, when moving a plant, or more so when transplanting an entire tree, it usually takes a long time for the animate being to adjust to the new place, e.g. to the specific soil, the air, the moisture, the light and its neighbours. Until the plant is able to adapt in its new environment, in particular to orientate itself newly towards the sunlight, takes time, so patience is needed. And the larger the plant/tree and the surrounding vegetation is, the longer it takes and the more challenging it is ! So if you have taken on that big new professional challenge in a large(r) organisation, give yourself the respective space, time and compassion. Sometimes 2 – 3 years could be needed for full adaptation !

In general when facing difficulties at work, it's important to keep sights on the horizon, on the mid- and long-term vision and goals. What was your plan in taking on the new position, and where would you like to be in 2, 5 or 10 years ? What you are experiencing today are building blocks on your path to the next level. Keep your sight on those goals and start implementing them now, today, tonight !

Figure 4 New palm tree (center) in the plantation

Volunteering

Take part in voluntary activities, associations. Besides being a good change of scenery, it can help you in your primary job. For example, take part in volunteer days at a charity, follow or be engaged in the staff association. Volunteering can be a source of inspiration, motivation and also networking.

****

_____ CHAPTER 12 _____

Documents, meetings

<u>Preparing a document etc.</u>

You are preparing a document, report or similar text and intend to share it in line with best practice with colleagues for comments ? Good ! Just be aware of that inner voice and feelings before doing so. Sometimes you may have this sense of uneasiness and/or insufficiency. Try to capture and personify it, and then reflect on it for a moment. What is it that is concretely bothersome ? Try to read and understand the inner message and identify its contents - the contours of it are usually already out there. If you succeed, immediately set about fixing or adjusting what is bothersome. You will feel that much better about your production and sending it out, and the feedback will respectively be more valuable and pertinent too.

This actually applies generally: if something appears irksome with your product, check it out and locate the cause. Ask your inner higher wisdom, and it will answer !

Sometimes significant formatting errors, typos etc. may also be symptomatic of larger issues in a document. Therefore, pay attention to these places and review respective contents. Readers will also be subconsciously drawn to these areas, and hence be particularly incentivised to provide (critical) comments on them.

By the way, if you or your staff are looking for information, exhaust or encourage to exhaust all means available prior to approaching / burdening other busy people in retrieving and forwarding that information. Oftentimes, the information is already available on a share drive, intranet, knowledge platforms, in past emails or even in the public domain, via e.g. a Google search. Similarly, you are intent on seeking advice from someone on a particular subject or issue occupying yourself ? Just put yourself in his/her place for a few moments and reflect. What would he/she likely say ? My guess is that in the majority of cases you would actually already be able to predict the answer fairly accurately by applying this method and therefore are not in need of the actual one. And as mentioned, no need to ask questions for demonstrating subordination !

Remaining flexible includes updating your own "final" version of critical documents, as needed, or at least entering respective notes on them. While you may not present an update now to others, you may do so later at opportune moment. As mentioned, most things are processes and not fixed for eternity. Unless you find yourself in very formal settings (e.g. formal disputes), do not fear possible ridicule, spite etc. in updating, besides the fact that others will not be viewing updates or corrections as critically as you may subjectively perceive them to be. It is always better to have a document in the public space that can stand over time than to be aware of having possibly created or sustained an inadequate production or worse, an "explosive" with a slow-burning fuse.

Circulated documents

There's usually a host of draft documents, papers, reports, communications in circulation, requesting comments, feedback etc. What a great opportunity to make yourself heard, to promote positions, to show engagement, or just to relieve boredom and increase your sense of self-worth. Read and comment on those documents. Even minor things are oftentimes appreciated, as the overall response rate from colleagues can be low. As in your general communications, phrase ideas and comments positively and constructively, rather than criticising. It's only a matter of practice.

In your feedback to a document, be concrete. Otherwise, only fluff is created. When you wish to suggest a correction / modification of a specific passage in a document, rather than just remarking "*para. 123 should be clearer and the issue of site readiness is missing*", say "*Para. 123 covers very important issues, but I would suggest to make it even clearer by also including the issue of site readiness, e.g. as follows:* [insert your revised version]". Your revised version is probably already more or less in your mind, so why not write it down ? Were you thinking the author of the document is waiting to volunteer as your ghostwriter and re-write the paragraph based on your appeal, while also meeting your standards and expectations ? Even if he/she did so, there would then be no second opportunity to fine-tune the text according to your ideas. Voluntary editing by the author may be rare, unless you are dealing with a supervisee or the counterpart (author) is particularly diligent, good-natured and empathetic. By providing concrete input, you also reduce the risk of being entirely ignored. It is hence better to go for the final product as desired, supplying ready-made plug-in material or at least attempt to do so. Any deviation would then be at the risk of the author.

You think the documents are too long (often 100s of pages with annexes) to review given the short deadline provided, oftentimes maybe just 1 – 2 days or COB (close of business) today ? You will be surprised how quickly you can grasp or get a general idea of the document, sometimes within minutes, just by looking at its structure, title and headings. Big picture remarks will immediately come to mind. Then, look at the passages most relevant to your work, oftentimes these are just a few. In this way, you may be done in less than 45 minutes, including sending off your remarks, with a great sense of fulfilment before you go home from work. Just do it ! And, what is more, you might just have thwarted an attempt by the author to pull a fast one on unsuspecting busy colleagues and/or departments in finalising a document to the author's advantage and to their detriment, by providing a short deadline to all for comments – a recurring tactic.

Meetings

Meetings are similarly a great opportunity for introducing yourself, getting involved, networking. If you are at a meeting, contribute if you have a thought or suggestion. Your voice will be heard, if not by the primary addressees, perhaps by some others who will get back to you in a positive way. Your contribution may not seem important to you, but once you start voicing it, it will sound important and most of the time it really is.

Particularly if you are new at an organisation, you may feel uneasy at first meetings. It's because you have not yet said anything in the round – after you have, the sense will disappear or diminish significantly. Oftentimes it will be easier to just add a comment or ask a question to start with.

For interventions at a meeting, raise your hand, make yourself noticeable or sometimes just start talking, as appropriate, very soon after you have the thought or question, otherwise someone else may voice that same thought or question of yours. In any case, do not wait patiently until voices have died down or there is a pause. This is not a theatre piece where the play director will give you the signal for your next line or to come on stage. Take the stage yourself, it's yours, as soon as the window of opportunity starts opening ! And afterwards, comment on the minutes, protocol – it is your chance to set or complete the record on your contribution.

If you are chairing the meeting and/or need to introduce and discuss a controversial topic, prepare your address and –

better – arrange for speakers to introduce or address various aspects of the topics, or just to ask questions. Spread out the burden and thereby also make the discussion more lively and interesting. Have points covered by alternates if the principals have become unpersuasive to the audience due to prior engagement on the topic.

There is the other side too: You may be invited and drawn into an excess of meetings. Many times your presence will actually be needed. But always check if you are able to decline without harm, to delegate or otherwise to only partially attend for relevant segments (with or without permission of the meeting organisers). In the worst case and if your full attention is not required in the meeting, draw on or develop your multi-tasking skills and accomplish some work during the meeting where possible.

It is good to raise issues, problems and make suggestions for improvements in public fora. However, be ready to then be called upon to implement the solution. If you do not have the space to take on these tasks, more restraint may be advisable in such, unless the points should be raised for other good reason, such as due to overall importance or to reinforce a preceding position taken.

This leads to other favourite types of phrases at meetings: The exclamation *"We should get more staff"*, *"the printer needs to be fixed"* or *"we should shorten the process"*. Who is "we", the kind, benevolent soul from next door ? Wishful thinking ! No, these expressions are often empty phrases and wastes of time. "We" is either yourself or someone concrete or a specific unit/department, which should be identified by name. Instead, it is therefore more productive and fair to say *"I think XYZ should be done and I am willing to volunteer for it"* or (if the unit/department is present) *"In regard to XYZ, may I suggest the ABC unit look into it and propose a solution"*, or otherwise *"I think XYZ is challenging in our current process, and I believe it could be best addressed by the ABC unit and its expertise in that area. If colleagues agree, I suggest that be recorded in the minutes and I would volunteer to go over the request with the unit and explain it to the colleagues."*

For virtual (online) meetings, there are both similarities and differences. Speaking up, for example, applies just the same. There is even the advantage that once you are given the floor, it may be harder to be interrupted. On the downside, people may therefore feel elevated and hog the online connection. There are also considerations as regards: speed of talking, which can again easily be either too slow or too fast; body language; background display; etiquette. A host of new literature is available on this topic[12].

Taking notes

If you are at a meeting with your boss or any other meeting in which you are told important things or in which you are inspired and/or have some good ideas, write them down. Are you really confident you would otherwise be remembering

---

[12] E.g. Dhawan, Erica. (2021) *Digital Body Language: How to Build Trust and Connection, No Matter the Distance*, St. Martin's Press.

all the follow-up or actions points, a few hours or days later ? Nothing worse than losing these precious, oftentimes irreproducible gains. And how embarrassing if your boss asks for an update later on and you are caught off guard and feel the need to cover up for the fact that you have quite forgotten about things, including and in particular the details of the conversation/discussion, irretrievably lost for all eternity.

Or, you are with a colleague discussing e.g. a difficult written response to a client, and together you are already skilfully phrasing important parts of the response, yet nobody is writing anything down while you are thinking and delivering. Wonderful, invaluable creations, made for the wind ! What a shame, and waste of valuable time. Going back to the office after the meeting (heroically having exclaimed beforehand "*I'll sit down and draft it*") and then embarking on crafting that letter – only to realise it means starting over or painfully back-tracking, or worst, having to re-enquire with your interlocutor ("*Do you remember what formulation we had agreed on for the final paragraph ?*"), is exemplary of office inefficiency.

If your discussion partners are supervised staff, ask them in such meetings whether they will be remembering the phrases when they are preparing a first draft of the letter/document. Hopefully they will thereby come to realise themselves the inefficiencies of the note-less approach. If need be, however, directly request your staff to note down the ideas which are in-the-making.

Laura, do you have a moment ?

Beware of those impromptu approaches after a meeting or in a corridor, or after a joint lunch/coffee, containing invitations or enquiries with a deceptive-type sense of closeness and familiarity:

> *"Laura, do you have a moment ?"*
>
> *"Hey Laura, would you have two minutes ?"*
>
> *"Could you just …?" / "Could I just .. ?"*

No, I don't / you can't ! You can oftentimes be sure that the conversation that is then to follow in the corridor or his/her office, and/or the assignment to be cast on you, may be more weighty or quite tough. For critical discussions, these may in the worst case potentially have long-term, maybe even treacherous or downright devastating consequences ("black swan event"). Therefore be attentive and, as appropriate, agreeable on principle, but ask kindly and respectfully what the meeting / action is about, and whether it's possible to schedule a meeting or revert for that purpose, as you now have another urgent assignment to work on, or meeting / phone call coming up and need to plan your day/week etc.

In *real* bilateral meetings, which can be sensitive or turn sensitive in the course of the meeting, take notes. Some information may become very important at a later stage.

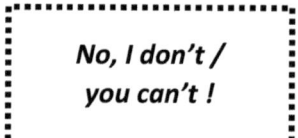

Resist being taken by surprise

Your notes, even scribblings, may be your only usable record of the meeting. If you had no paper/pen at hand during the meeting, sit down afterwards and quickly note down the main points from memory. If pressed for time, you can expand on the points later.

Should you have been mistreated, misunderstood or should otherwise be dissatisfied with a meeting, you can write a post scriptum by email to your counterpart(s) communicating your concerns, corrections or other dissatisfaction. If you have admitted to something rashly or inadvertently in the meeting, and this was on reflection not justified, or have taken the blame for something unnecessarily, rectify or place it in context as necessary. The email may seem embarrassing or discomforting at first, but it can bring relief and help in the mid- and long-term in preventing worse from happening. It is also important for general wellbeing to free yourself of such negativity.

****

_____ CHAPTER 13 _____

Filing

Information should be organised in such way that it is instantly accessible, and with that is meant in a matter of seconds or minutes. Keep it simple ! In the hectic daily office rush, anything longer will basically render the information useless most of the time. Therefore, documents and materials should be filed away in a manageable number of paper or electronic folders or similar means (knowledge platforms etc.). Your unit/department will also have filing guidelines. Sometimes these can be quite strict, but then oftentimes not followed in practice.

Since many documents and materials are (still) contained as attachments in emails, the email filing system is critical. A most basic but effective system is to archive emails on a quarterly or half-yearly basis. For work in the running quarter, maintain some general files and only few, not more than perhaps half a dozen or maximally a dozen special folders. Anything more will quickly become too complex and unpractical to manage and use under daily pressures. Emails within folders can then be sorted by author/addressee and

GETTING THAT EXPAT JOB IN INT'L. DEV. AND ADVANCING ○ 112

date, and/or searched well by keyword. Emails that need to be actioned (and cannot be dealt with immediately) can either be red-flagged or moved to an "Inbox act" or similar folder.

A special folder I would recommend is "Resources", containing any important or basic information that requires frequent consultation. It may e.g. contain the latest version of a particular manual, the unit's latest organigramme, instructions on using some application, equipment etc. The Resources folder can be carried forward from one work and archive period to the next.

Make good use of rule functionality of your email system. E.g. all emails in which you are only copied should be directly deposited in a CC folder. Similarly, announcements, internal news, daily briefs etc. could go into a Circular mail folder.

An email folder partitioning (derived from the main Inbox) can be recommended as shown on the next page.

In your quarterly or half-yearly archives, maintain - as for the daily emails - only few key sub-folders, perhaps half a dozen or a dozen, though exceptions prove the rule.

It is good practice to separate personal emails and documents from official ones from the onset. This would avoid having to sort through 1000s of emails and hundreds of documents if you ever leave your position and need to hand over files to a successor. You may also be pressed for time at that moment, resulting in inadequate or incomplete

* Inbox act
* CC
* Pending (if need be, a "Pending secondary" can be used too)
* For printing
* Special Project (but max only 5 – 6 of these types of folders)
* Circular mails
* Resources
* Temporary
* Personal
* Archive
* Archive CC

Figure 5 Email folders

sorting. Try to therefore write and receive personal emails only from/in your personal email account.

For more personal-type notes from meetings, on reports etc., keep these in a separate folder or record them in a separate notebook.

Parallel to this, a basic notebook, compendium or e-file/dashboard containing all critical administrative/technical information comes in very handy too. It should list e.g. essential telephone numbers, passwords for applications and codes for machines (only in encrypted form), helpdesks/helplines, budget codes, recurring deadlines, key statistical data (e.g. number of staff, offices, clients, turnover, budget, performance data), titles/sources of key manuals and regulations, official holidays etc., for quick and easy access. Such notebook or e-file can also be very conveniently taken along to meetings or having available at online meetings, particularly those called on short notice. For e-files, however, beware of the risk of out-of-battery scenarios or other technical issues, and/or possible inappropriateness of consulting electronic devices during critical in-person meetings.

For documents and materials managed other than through emails, e.g. in (shared) knowledge platforms, document repositories or other resource management tools, the same organisational principles as outlined above apply. Ensure easy access, limit the number of folders / sub-folders, make use of technical functionalities (ordering, flagging and sorting), and keep it simple.

****

_____ CHAPTER 14 _____

Managing a team

If you are leading a team, managing a section or otherwise have supervisory functions, my recommendation is to make good use of the known, effective tools available for organising and monitoring work:

- ❖ Strategic Plans (Strategies)
- ❖ Workplans (Operational Plans)
- ❖ Individual performance objectives, Terms of Reference
- ❖ Accountabilities
- ❖ Organigramme
- ❖ Service Level Agreements (SLAs)
- ❖ Standard Operating Procedures (SOPs)
- ❖ Key Performance Indicators (KPIs)
- ❖ Regular Team Meetings
- ❖ Retreats

Strategic Plans (short-, medium and long-term) should be established in consultative and inclusive (participatory) manner among team members and with stakeholders, following a retreat. The Plans should contain high-level objectives, broken down into mid-level or further, more detailed objectives. The PESTEL analysis[13] will be helpful in determining the context of operations.

Workplans are derived from the Strategic Plans, the Organisation's Mission Statement and vision. Strategic Plans establish actions, responsible actor(s), timelines, KPIs, methods for measuring the indicators, data sources and comments. The Workplan, usually established on an annual or bi-annual basis, should be updated as needed.

In a next step and cascading further down, performance objectives of staff are aligned or updated in accordance with the Workplan. Where necessary, Terms of Reference are established for new staff or adjusted (respecting internal procedures) for existing staff.

Establishing accountabilities of sub-units or other management entities helps to avoid overlap, operational gaps and to manage expectations, thereby also avoiding potential disagreement. SLAs among entities can complement the set of accountabilities. SLAs certainly help to achieve clarity, however they may sometimes be inadequate to capture the real-time dynamics of team work, which oftentimes require extensive back-and-forth to finally

---

[13] Method for determining the Political, Economic, Sociological, Technological, Environmental and Legal environment of Operations, see e.g.
https://www.cipd.co.uk/knowledge/strategy/organisational-development/pestle-analysis-factsheet#gref,
https://en.wikipedia.org/wiki/PEST_analysis.

achieve an outcome. SLAs which are too rigid, e.g. foreseeing only one-time process execution without feedback loops and iterations, and/or which are applied too rigidly, will instead in fact be hindering operations and are likely to lead to superfluous, additional disputes on the SLAs themselves.

SOPs for all work processes and aligned with the needs of the Workplan, may be arduous at first to produce. However, while not only satisfying quality management standards (Total Quality Management – TQM, ISO Certification or similar), they do help significantly in resolving or preventing disputes within the Team as to how to manage the work, who is doing what and defining or confirming relevant accountabilities. The processes also help in promoting or raising visibility of a unit/section, or in institutional restructuring exercises.

In the corporate sector, a compendium of SOPs may be significant in company takeovers, constituting an intangible asset and reflective of a going concern.

Sometimes there may be a tendency for management, leadership or other higher level decision-making processes to be excluded from SOP collections, for various reasons, e.g. a process allegedly being *"too difficult"*, *"too complex"* or that it *"does not lend itself for an SOP"*. In reality possibly just the wish to evade accountability may be the reason behind such tendency. However, while not only ensuring transparency of operations, identifying, establishing and formulating these processes in SOPs actually help to ensure rigour of thought, logic, effectiveness and appropriateness of the processes. And once having embarked on textualizing such process, I would hold that in all cases the steps and considerations of those high-level processes can in fact be well captured on paper/screen, and that this actually facilitates execution and soundness of the underlying operations for the future. The EU is exemplary in this regard, setting out in extensive detail including definitions e.g. the risk assessment process and risk communication in food safety matters[14].

Recognizing and understanding team dynamics is an important skill as a manager. This includes awareness of when to step back on issues or in ongoing developments of a team.

Arriving at team ownership, buy-in by its members, is a most valuable asset, a great accomplishment in no way to be taken for granted, setting the ground for individual and joint excellence and performance. Empowerment of team members, delegation of authority paired with accountability, are key building blocks for buy-in.

Knowledge sharing in teams is essential, though it should not mean moving in lockstep on all matters. This would bear the risk of slowing down matters unnecessarily or even bringing them to a halt. Instead, a sufficient degree of trust should be arrived at in a team, enabling its members to have space for individual performance, and for sharing their planning and

---

[14] Reg. (EU) 2019/1381 of 20 June 2019 on the transparency and sustainability of the EU risk assessment in the food chain (Transparency Regulation).

outcomes as appropriate and necessary from time to time (need-to-know-basis), then ideally positively welcomed and reinforced by co-team members in synergistic way.

Regular team meetings are essential for effective management, e.g. once a week, every fortnight or at least every month. A meeting plan covering the whole year – subject to adjustment as called for – will be very useful in this regard (see example overleaf). As mentioned above, communication in all its forms is key to managing a team, and team meetings are an essential element of that. If you have a large team, additional meetings with sub-team leaders will regularly be helpful too.

Team retreats from time to time are similarly instrumental in reflecting on the past, taking stock of the present with its successes and challenges, and charting or confirming the way forward.

Moving between the collective (group meetings) and the individual (bilateral meetings) is a good technique, and learning when to employ one and the other(s), including meta-levels of meeting composition, and applying such in practice, is a most valuable skill. For example, meeting separately with administration and/or other support staff can provide much needed insight.

At the same time, meeting-creep and holding meetings just for the sake of holding them, without real content and/or avoiding the important issues, is a waste of organisational and personal resources, aside from demotivating staff and

Team Meetings 2022

Dep./Office \ Month	Jan	Feb	Mar	...	Oct	Nov	Dec	Comments
HQ	Wed 05	Wed 02	Wed 02		Wed 05	Wed 02	Wed 07	Monthly: HQ Mgmt Team
HQ			Tue 15				Tue 20	Quarterly: HQ Mgmt+X
HQ			Thu 17					Semi-annual: All
Field/Agency A			Thu 17					Semi-annual: All
Field/Agency B						Thu 17		Semi-annual: All
Field/Agencies A,B,C							Fri 09	Annual: All

Table 12 Team Meetings Schedule Example

causing frustration. Therefore, have the courage to adjust meetings as necessary, e.g. shortening, combining meetings or devising other appropriate formats for meetings and further modulating these as needed. Consistent awareness of and orientation to the objectives and overall mission of the unit and organisation are very helpful in this regard. Beware also of the unfortunate practice of directing participants' attention to secondary "theaters", a common technique employed by some to avoid accountability on primary issues. E.g. directing discussion to the caterer/cafeteria and its meal plan or other non-strategic topic, knowing well this will syphon oxygen off other subjects for the rest of the meeting.

If you have returned unsatisfactory work to a team member with your comments on it, it is advisable to make a copy for your files beforehand. Alternatively, summarise your comments in a follow-on email. Again, these records may - or hopefully may not - be needed at another point. Also, the comments are very valuable in establishing and writing up best practice, e.g. in an SOP.

When employing staff and/or adding members to a team, resist the temptation to attempt to replicate role models in the team (including yourself, as "Mini-Me" clones). Instead, value diverseness and ensure complementarity of skills, ideas and qualities, for mutual gains and excelling together.

****

_____ CHAPTER 15 _____

Travel and holidays

Travelling

Travels are usually a positive enrichment of your job. It gives opportunity to grow your network, get to know colleagues and counterparts also a bit more personally and in your free time to experience some new or yet unknown surroundings. It also allows escape from the daily office grind for some time. Some individuals may appear to wish to use travel in order to spend the smallest possible proportion of their time in office (hoping maybe thereby to minimise work and office interaction, essentially becoming a "paid tourist"), while in the other extreme others may prefer to hunker down in their offices as much as possible, shutting the door to the outside world, and to minimise any interaction. Much better is to see and experience the travel for what it is: a work mission to and at another location, with a change of scenery.

Getting a self-initiated travel off the ground is sometimes not so easy. You typically need to write terms of reference, and they may not seem sufficient or convincing. Tip: use the laws of coagulation. Cluster the travel around a nucleus of an activity that is fixed and secure. Then, expand by contacting colleagues at the destination, informing them of your intended visit and interest in meeting them to discuss X, Y and Z. There are usually always topics to discuss. Most of the time, responses are likely to be positive, even if concrete commitments cannot yet be made due to concurring events etc. But this is sufficient for entering the planned meetings and topics into the terms of reference as bilateral meetings. If specific counterparts are not yet clear, refer to the unit/department. Structure your draft schedule so that you will have time for some expansions or additions.

Just before leaving and as you arrive, pick up all loose ends and reach out again to those from whom you have not yet been able to get responses. The imminent arrival can work wonders in convincing and livening up people, this is a human trait. And when you have arrived in the office at your destination, continue with your efforts, seeking out colleagues at their workplaces etc. Meet colleagues in the entrance hall, corridors, kitchens, at the elevator, in the cafeteria. Also, spontaneously attend any meetings and events that you hear of, just show up if permissible. Or, assemble colleagues spontaneously for a meeting if they have been unable to organise such themselves due to busyness, internal disagreements or other reason such as plain disorganisation.

It can happen that in your meetings at the destination you may be at a loss what to say. Either due to lack of preparation, spontaneity of the meeting or just plain travel

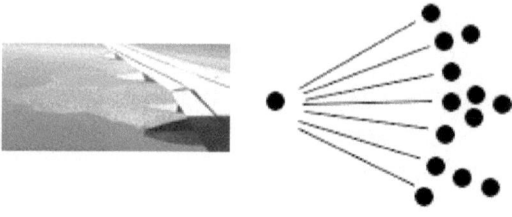

Figure 6 Travel and meetings

fatigue. To avoid embarrassment and make good use of time, ask questions and associate ideas. Counterparts will often be happy to explain and expand on their work. This will then most likely also coax out your own (forgotten) value, and you will start remembering things which can be of interest for your counterparts. Before you know it, you will have a lively conversation going, producing results and valuable points to be followed up on.

And if there are language barriers in meetings or interactions, with no translator available, paying attention to tone of voice, context of the conversation, timing and sequencing of insertions and contributions by participants, facial expression and body language, may prove to be useful. You may actually be able to understand much more than you or your counterparts may think possible.

Write your travel report as soon as possible. Best, already during your stay or on your way back, while events and thoughts are still fresh in your mind. If you met colleagues spontaneously and talked about some work issues, enter this into the report too. Circulate your travel report as widely as possible. Again, this is your opportunity to make yourself known and shine.

Holidays

Your rest is well deserved ! Take holidays when and as needed. Do not postpone holidays too long – burnout can creep in unnoticed at first, and before you know it can cause greater harm with longer term implications.

However, some colleagues might just be waiting for you to be on that holiday, giving them a chance to do things according to their wishes or to revert to old ways of doing things. Some may be out to downright sabotage your work while you are away. Others may just be careless, negligent, indifferent. Therefore, it is prudent to keep an eye on your work area during your absence, even if only from a distance and perhaps only every one to two days. Ask to be copied and kept in the loop, and intervene as necessary.

Be wary of any periods of silence in which you would normally have expected some feedback on an issue or activity. This is just the time when things might be developing negatively, cooking up, and/or some scheming could be in the making or already in effect to shift blame, in the worst case to you, to be discovered with a time delay. Of course, being vigilant may detract from your holiday experience, but it could potentially save several weeks and months of repair work upon your return, if indeed things can actually be rectified.

****

_____ CHAPTER 16 _____

Performance reports

An exercise both managers and supervisees may regularly be less keen about is the periodic performance reporting. This is actually unfortunate, since if done constructively in genuine way, performance evaluations can be a very good tool for individuals to excel on all levels, to reach their potential, and also for the manager to reflect, learn and make adjustments where indicated.

Usually the process begins with a self-assessment, followed by a personal meeting, before the manager provides a written assessment, which ideally is shared with the supervisee in draft form first for comments. Ordinarily there is a mid-term and a final, annual assessment. Oftentimes these may be done with substantial delay, procrastinated by both sides.

Diligent preparation is the key to these exercises. As a supervisee, it is useful to collect all information about your work performed, training and any other work-related activities in the reporting period. You will need this for your self-assessment, but also for the personal meeting. It is best to do this chore on a monthly basis from the start, since a last-minute collection can be overwhelming, requiring many hours of work at inopportune time. A good way is to first write down what easily comes to mind, followed by a diligent review of emails, calendars, files and archived documents. Yes, you may have 1000s of emails, however when focussing on the "sent" emails, and among those on main counterparts, foremost your manager, it should normally be possible to capture the majority of your value actions / outputs fairly rapidly. This is also why filing emails and documents by quarterly or half-yearly periods including key sub-folders can be very helpful.

The material for the performance report and the performance report itself can also feed in well to your CV, updating it as necessary. For competency-based interviews, they will help too in identifying suitable examples. So, the performance report fortunately does have other benefits.

A further good side effect of collecting materials for your performance report is that if you were ever e.g. to consider publishing or posting an article, contribution or similar, related to your work area (in keeping with its regulations), you will be able to identify and retrieve materials more easily or also come up with ideas for publishing in the first place. Oftentimes the substance or concepts are in fact lying there right in front of you, just needing identification, contextualisation and commentary.

Your factual representation of achievements will be key to presenting and defending an objective and holistic view of your performance. E.g. if your coordination skills are criticised, perhaps the assessment was only based on interaction with a particular group, and did not consider your extensive and effective coordination with other groups or counterparts ? Make it a point to identify and express your achievements. This includes routine activities, which in their aggregation during the reporting period may be a substantial achievement, e.g. "cleared 750 financial transactions" or "reviewed and authorised about 250 work orders" or "organised and chaired X meetings on Y". Where you are not sure of the number, estimate using reasonable indicators.

In general, try not to let yourself be intimidated and avoid becoming defensive, angered or irritated in the face of criticism - this could also just play into a manager's game, if existent. For example, a manager could just be trying to provoke or "have a go" at a supervisee for a competency or issue as a proxy for something else which he/she is unable or unwilling to formulate. Therefore, listen carefully and try to understand and reflect on the issues raised. Distinguish between facts and non-facts, hearsay, speculation etc., consider context, and separate facts from analysis and judgement.

In exceptional cases, it could be advantageous from a psychological standpoint to help the manager express his/her criticism if he/she is having difficulty in doing so and therefore unnecessary tension is created in the process. However, as the performance report is a formal process with potential consequences, this technique should be applied with restraint and always remains subject to one's own best judgement, guided in the first instance by the precautionary principle. It could only e.g. be applicable where one is quite sure of one's position and hence prepared to hear or accept the criticism - particularly if it is evident, has been justifiably expressed priorly or is negligible -, and/or one has a compelling defense ready, or a possible counter-charge for which it is worth entering the discussion.

People frequently have the tendency to narrow sights on smaller or one-off (perceived) negative instances, be it when considering a set of actions, projects, relationships or, as discussed here, performance periods, and in doing so to negate and obscure the big picture. Therefore, make sure in the discussion and reflection to try to always get back to the broader view of your performance, as any reasonable outsider would see it. Surely the performance in that broader scope of matters was overall not so bad, in fact pretty good ? A soccer goalie has maybe made 1000 saves, but is criticised for not preventing 10 scores. Do not be unduly hard on yourself and/or take blame and negativity where not indicated and accepted by your infallible inner compass.

If you have brought discrepancies to the attention of your manager, but should this have been in vain and/or you remain feeling unfairly assessed in the performance report(s), or wrongly treated in the process, you can use the formal tools and systems available to you. These can range from a) simply providing a counterview or writing a rebuttal in the report (but accepting the report as such), b) indicating your disagreement with the report in the checkbox usually provided for that, and then bringing the disagreement to the attention of a dedicated performance review body/unit (usually located within the Human Resources/HR Department), c) filing a complaint with an internal oversight department and/or d) submitting a claim or application under formal dispute resolution (board of appeal or similar entity, court). During this time, which can extend to months/years, your report may oftentimes not be finalised or confirmed, which may be advantageous if/when you are seeking another position elsewhere.

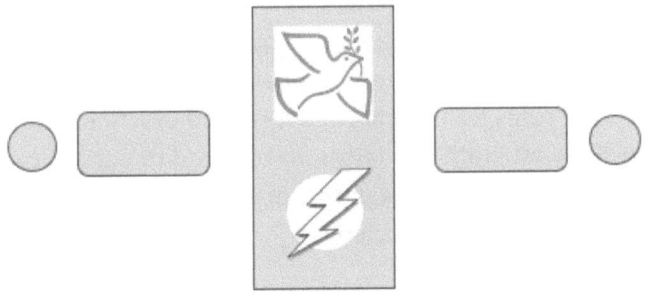

Figure 7 Performance report meeting

****

_____ CHAPTER 17 _____

The dark side

If/when you are approached with doubtful ventures, requests or propositions, undue pressures, expressing your concerns is both legitimate and advisable, and should be done in a collected, respectful, but firm, factual manner, referring as necessary to workplans, priorities, mandates, principles, rules, values etc., and it is good practice to copy in other relevant staff. The latter, as referred to earlier, can be very effective in exposing and stopping collusion, ill-begotten secrecy and other unethicalness.

Similarly, do not believe, spread or sustain gossip. Do not engage in unnecessary chatter. Stay with reliable, preferably first-hand information and facts, which will carry matters much farther in the long-term and moreover enables you to be at peace with yourself. For the UN, the Guide for UN Staff is an excellent resource on ethics and the workplace[15].

_____

[15] UN Ethics Office, *Putting Ethics to Work, A Guide for UN Staff* (2012/2017), available at

If asked for evaluations or comments about colleagues ("*Is so-and-so doing a good job ?*", "*Is X performing ?*", "*Is Y competent ?*", *What do you think of Z ?*"), best would be to indicate that this is addressed in the scope of performance discussions. Do not let yourself be lured into any off-the-cup assessment or remark, also or particularly if the request comes from the hierarchy. Resist the momentary flattery that your opinion is ostensibly valued, or any managerial pressure to disclose internal contemplations, keeping in mind that managers come and go and as a rule do not own an organisation / company. Aside from the breach of confidentiality, labelling people who have been working for months or years with some casual epithets in passing is both disrespectful to the concerned and usually inaccurate, not doing justice, potentially in fact causing serious harm and grief to the concerned. Shortened assessments may also be used for covert HR planning. HR issues should be dealt with only in their proper context and according to established HR rules and guidelines.

As you have obtained cruising speed in your new job, there may be further attempts to derail you and your vehicle. Again, who said the new job would be a bed of roses ? The attempts could be direct onslaughts or take more subtle forms.

Direct assaults are usually best dealt with in the same way as criticism raised in a performance meeting/report, as set out

---

https://www.un.org/en/ethics/assets/pdfs/Attachment_2_EN_Putting%20Ethics%20to%20Work.pdf above, identifying facts, data, context, analysis/judgement etc. Sometimes a simple, harmless "rude him/her back" may work too. However, decisions of principle may need to be made as to a) whether a standard "on deck" toolkit for countering is sufficient, b) whether and with whom to engage in such discussion in the first place, i.e. to possibly involve others, or to attempt to move the discussion to another context, and c) whether this is a one-off instance or systemic issue, requiring different potential approaches.

On all unethicalness brought one's ways, any encouragement of breach of rules, transgressions, involvement in conspiracies, bad-mouthing etc., it would as mentioned be recommendable to push back politely, but determinedly and promptly on these. Stand up for your principles and morality. Involve other colleagues/units as necessary. If in doubt, ask for instructions in writing. Push back also helps in avoiding feeling down due to absorbing such negativity.

However, in living this approach, effort should be made to try to avoid being a nuisance or seen as a trouble-maker. Instead, best is just to express your position and note down, date and record such behaviour brought toward you, basically like a journalist, and copy and file any related documents too – these could be needed at a later point.

"Passing the buck" (responsibility), "shifting the monkey"[16] (tasks, burdens), i.e. playing musical chairs, delegating back

---

[16] Whitaker, Todd. (2014) *Shifting the Monkey: The Art of Protecting Good People From Liars, Criers, and Other Slackers (A*

up to the line manager are among the more harmless forms of office mischief.

More sophisticated attempts at derailment would be for example leveraging outside "allies" (e.g. institutes, media outlets) to deliver a blow (be it imagined) on the inside. It may be difficult or hazardous to put a stop to such "enemy within" and therefore it can be more prudent, if reasonable and containable, to resort as above to communicating the facts, setting the record straight etc., and avoid being triggered. Similarly, false flag operations could be instituted, with few, or at least no accessible traces to the originator. Here, awareness would be the first step in countering such schemes, followed by further steps as referenced above, dependent on circumstances and resources available.

In your daily work, try to be vigilant to not lightly provide approvals, clearances, sign memos etc. that you know you should preferably not, or where you know you should at least be taking more time in order to review the item or file and secure any necessary adjustments that will allow the action to stand over time. This applies in particular when starting out on a new job. People may attempt to take advantage of the situation and pull a fast one. At the same time, try to ensure as above that you are not seen as an obstructionist or superfluous decelerator. In any case, with such applied due diligence, you can calmly face all regular or unexpected debates/disputes, audits, investigations, reports etc.

---

book on school leadership and teacher performance), Solution Tree.

Undermining and removal of work areas/functions

If your work or function is being undermined, reached through or not respected, on the quiet or overtly, against agreed divisions of work, a first step would be to acknowledge this to yourself. It's common to deny this to oneself, to preserve self-respect and self-esteem. However, do not allow yourself to accept the transgressions and "a stitch in time saves nine". You may believe or sway yourself into believing that you are granting the perpetrators a "favour" or demonstrating particular loyalty, especially if these are in your reporting line, if you accept and remain quiet, and that you will even eventually be rewarded for the humiliation and suffering that you are enduring. No, better to get real.

Best would be to thematise the undermining and reach-through with those responsible and ask for cessation. Present and praise your work/the team's work and call in the acknowledgement at suitable occasions. If you are a manager and it were found that a member of your team were colluding in the undermining, it might be difficult to address this, as inside linkages ("spies" in subordinated teams) may have been nested since a long time and the staff member may on the surface be well able to claim to just be following instructions from the hierarchy. However, it could prove effective to record carefully and consider bringing to his/her attention any under-performance originating from him/her and being the result of cutting corners and passing over you. You are after all still his/her functional supervisor, with respective qualification, and responsible for assessments etc.

Yet, if the undermining and other transgression continued and/or became more serious, there may be no choice but to raise the issue at higher levels or with other responsible departments/units. Transgressions can also be relevant for performance evaluations, i.e. being able to refer to areas that have become outside of your control or staff that you are no longer able to supervise, and for which you respectively can and should therefore no longer be held accountable.

Transgressions and tacit removal of work areas could indeed bear the risk that one officially remains accountable for the results of the wiped tasks/areas, or is seen as such, and may be blamed for any ensuing related underperformance or mishaps, also in linked areas under or near one's control.

In the worst case, this could even be the scheme behind such (case of harassment/mobbing): grabbing some organisational jewels ("poaching"), while conveniently arranging for a scapegoat in case things go wrong in an area where the transgressors are not really experts. This is unacceptable, therefore it is recommended to speak out in such case and make clear that this calls for cessation. An only exception could be where it is already clear that failure of the venture is ahead, and the mischief-makers will be taking the hit, then it could be consequential to step aside and let them fail ("*vous avez voulu*"), and insist on returning to proper order afterwards in light of the occurrences.

If exceptionally the reach-throughs, the use of one's or the team's assets were unavoidable, or indeed were actually found to be for the good of the organisation, it should be ensured that one has agreed on the terms and conditions, be it after the fact, in particular the precise scope and duration, and any compensation. All else failing, one can set out one's understanding unasked, unilaterally, in writing. If possible, it would be favourable to negotiate having oneself/the team work in a timed subcontracting arrangement with other units/departments, rather than giving up resources entirely at the behest of others.

It must be said that sometimes the reach-throughs might not occur from actual malice, but out of a type of listless wandering, or ignorance of the pilferers, identifying ostensible "easy tasks", oftentimes plainly visible lesser tasks, while neglecting actual ones. This would e.g. be the case of an executive attending to receipts instead of pursuing resource mobilization or public relations. In this case, politely advising the concerned that there is no need to address X or Y, or that he/she can be relieved from this task, as this is what one is employed to do, and will be content to continue to do, could work. The concerned may not have even realised how he/she had veered off from his/her job description, and will be grateful for the advice.

A sequel to undermining and removal of work areas would be the – hopefully rare - phenomenon of deliberately unduly removing a work area or resource from a staff member or unit/department, only to later, after protest, return it, expecting appreciation and praise for the 'good deed' (and being taken aback if such is not extended). This appears as a technique of wishing to simultaneously both instil fear and gain favour with the concerned. This is overall mischievous behaviour or worse, depending on the extent and pattern of practice, a devious game !

New strategies, restructuring

Major moves to eliminate posts, units, departments or to just dismiss certain staff could come in disguise as well. New departmental / organisational strategies, preceded by consultant studies and/or authored by a task force, leadership team etc., could exemplify such approach. Ample jurisprudence documents such possible modus operandi[17].

If you found yourself to be potentially affected by these, you are not powerless, and procedures are usually long-drawn, giving you also time for personal planning. Staff consultation and consideration are almost always a must, and there will be procedures laid out for the change process. A violation of these principles and rules/regulations can render the plan null and void. In the public sector and even in most commercial businesses, as mentioned usually no single person "owns" your organisation. And even if so, the regulatory and legal environments, and lastly shareholders/stakeholders, publicity and the public at large,

---

[17] E.g. at https://www.un.org/en/internaljustice/undt/judgments-orders.shtml;
https://www.ilo.org/dyn/triblex/triblexmain.advancedSearch?p_l ang=en; https://curia.europa.eu/juris/recherche.jsf?language=en.

provide for a host of limitations and valuable checks and balances. This means pursuing and safeguarding the public interest, and the external involvement is for the public good.

In a restructuring or similar exercise, plain common sense, logic and facts which can be found on the intranet/internet, in reports (internal, external), strategic documents etc., can be allies. What are the desired changes, have these been properly identified, formulated and studied (feasibility analysis), and importantly, are they measurable ? Are data and measurement metrics in place before the change ("As Is" state), and provisions made to collect data and undertake measurements after the change ("To Be" state) and of course to share these with all concerned, in transparent way ?

New strategies may be presented at inconvenient times, in passing in the context of other meetings, or just by inconspicuous email circulation, with short or unclear response times. Strategies may be presented with a sense of "imminent success", undeserving of any questioning and basically discouraging any suggested amendments or deeper consideration. In any event, better to not let yourself become dazzled by any of these cheap manoeuvres. Attend the meetings, articulate your concerns, contribute to discussion walls/boards and encourage also colleagues to do so, respond to documents in circulation, indicating if necessary that your comments are provisional due to the short lead time, and/or request an extension, but be prepared in any case to submit at least key points or bullets by the original deadline given. Do not remain silent – then manipulators have succeeded !

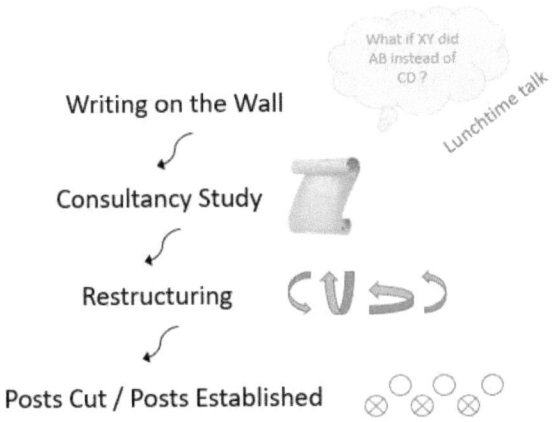

Figure 8 Restructuring: possible pivotal stages affecting employees

Restructurings could also come in the guise of temporary arrangements, to which one may be agreeable out of complacency, indifference or due to the ostensible transitory nature. However, as seen in the course of history generally, temporary arrangements oftentimes become and/or are indeed intended to become permanent.

If you were to sense the restructuring may affect your position, and in all other cases where you may sense you or your position could be at risk, it would be good to ensure that you have archived and backed-up your work regularly, as described earlier, as a matter of precaution for ready access in case of informal or formal dispute. Equally, it would be prudent to compile relevant (staff) regulations, rules, policies, guidance documents and other organisational materials that may be essential in such case for rapid access, as well as ensuring that contracts, salary statements, training certificates, onboarding documentation and other personal records are available, particularly if these materials are only accessible from internal systems. Due foresight pays off.

If you are at the other end and you were to need to implement a new strategy as a manager: Be open, introduce the new (draft) concept in transparent way, ask for comments and address these in rational manner, record results in writing (minutes). Valid comments should be incorporated and questionable ones disproven. Do not block or shy away from discussions, whatever their nature – these reach their natural bottom ground once all issues are on the table and have been genuinely considered. Plan and schedule the stages of strategy development and implementation, ensuring that sufficient time is given for expressing and integrating input, making necessary adjustments. Once again, communication to all concerned would be key in introducing and realising new strategies.

For major projects, facilitation by external resources would be advisable, and organisation of retreats, workshops and similar public discussion fora. Change processes need time, should be respectful and inclusive, and open to adjustment in order to be successful. As a manager, you are the steward of processes, structures and resources, but only with the greater good in mind and being guided in service of this in participatory way, can lasting, positive results be achieved.

Some strategies and reorganisations could be introduced by disinformation. Repeated claims could for instance be put out that a unit/department will e.g. be handling customer service in future, that staff ABC will be moving to another unit/department, or that HQ has agreed. In such case one would rightly question: Really, when was this decided, by whom ? Were these persons authorized, was due process followed, and has this been produced or recorded in writing ? The tactic of manipulators would be that through repeating voicing and presenting the change as a given, it becomes so omnipresent and sure that ultimately it is seen as a reality and the responsible officials thereupon would see no choice but to confirm or approve the change. The change has thus been predetermined by way of repetition. Therefore, again, best to avoid being misled by such creeping, clandestine moves. Question the issues and claims, request documentation and raise your concerns as you see fit.

Another tool could be staff surveys with a hidden agenda of targeting certain processes, structures or particular staff. Though here also there are effective ways of countering such move. The survey will or must usually still go through a consultation process, where scope, contents and goals of the survey are discussed, and therefore respective feedback can be given, verbal and in writing. Where such feedback is ignored, results of the survey can then legitimately be questioned.

Luckily also, the outcome of such surveys would in reality never really be predictable, and what is more, results could lead to new/other insights, besides not confirming, or even contradicting the originally malignly intended outcomes !

Audits and as mentioned consultancy studies for restructurings could be misused to achieve underlying, unwritten objectives. If this is sensed, effective possible measures would be to identify and state the specific points or concepts where the audit or expert study is factually incorrect, illogical, incoherent or inconsistent or otherwise defies professional standards and/or organisational values. Attempting to bend a banana straight will always fail, and such bending would regularly be attempted and be evident where other motives are at play, and so it would be a matter of identifying and exposing those inherent flaws.

For support in countering unwarranted audits etc. there are resources available, such as colleagues who are of the same opinion, staff association, ombudsperson, ethics office, and other oversight bodies or authorities within or outside an organisation. Any ill-intended audit, malicious investigation / prosecution etc. should be called out and brought to attention of the mentioned entities and any other responsible authorities. When addressed as a collective and/or several institutions and persons are involved, righteousness should almost always prevail over time.

Harassment, mobbing

Should you be subjected to harassment or mobbing, early intervention will be the best recipe, at the first signs. Definitely preferable is not to wait for matters to accumulate. The only exceptions would be to a) collect more evidence in order to make a better case, but that could be a risky strategy and may also be held against oneself for having been inactive or b) picking your battles, i.e. letting things go for the moment, as you might also need to consider the time available and economise on your energy. And while support from others may also be beneficial, a) it might not be possible to secure such for all interventions or not at all times due to absences etc. and b) sometimes (temporary) firewalling of the case could be preferable. Nevertheless, at the same time one would have to be careful about applicable time limits, statutes of limitations (e.g. 180 days for harassment claims, 90 days for requests for administrative review, frequently less). The ombudsperson or neutral workplace advisors, if available, may in any case be good initial contact points.

Sometimes offenders might not even realise that the concerned person is feeling harassed or indeed is harassed by their actions. That is why addressing the situation openly would be important. Sometimes things can be fixed at this early stage. The onus would then be on oneself to explain to counterparts what is offensive and, most importantly, how one views that interactions should be occurring. If you would e.g. feel uncomfortable about people commenting on your clothes and this is not part of the permissible, unavoidable or expected organisational culture, i.e. expecting colleagues to accept such and join in, then express your misgivings to the concerned, kindly requesting cessation. In so doing, it would be important to direct the focus to your sentiments rather than the offensive actions/actor. Comments might have been made genuinely in good intention or just thoughtlessly, or in unawareness of organisational regulations. In such cases the concerned would probably be thankful for the advice and things would be resolved to everyone's satisfaction very quickly, if not instantly.

A somewhat amusing while still obviously annoying case, modified here for illustration purposes from a comparable one recounted from expat life, would be that of a coworker having the habit of sniffing each time he/she would pass by another colleague's (open door) office on the corridor. It could be a small thing, but one could imagine that if it would happen every day and on each occasion of passing by, it could understandably then become quite disturbing, akin to water drop torture. The displayed habit could be a subconscious attempted demonstration of imagined power, an insecurity, or even deliberate irritation of the other colleague, who knows ?

What to reasonably do in such case ? A first step in any case would be to observe and confirm the pattern, ensuring "there's a there there". If so, the second step would of course be more delicate and depend on many circumstances, both organisational and individual. Perhaps a diplomatic third way out, avoiding petty office skirmishes where possible, could be preferable in such type of situation, e.g. by setting up a soundscape such as a small waterfall machine or other white noise emitter, close by the office door, to disperse sounds.

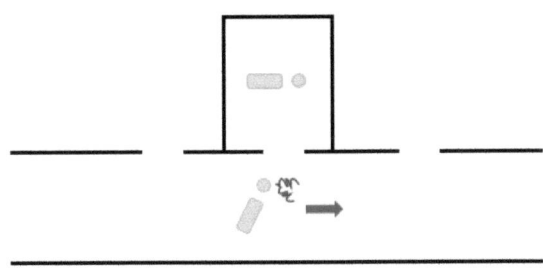

Figure 9 Harassment by sniffing on the corridor

Sometimes there could also be a process/procedural background to offending actions or typical scenarios leading to the offensive action. In this case drawing up a draft Standard Operating Procedure (SOP) related to your work area, or an amendment to an existing SOP, and sharing this for comments with your interlocutors and manager, would be both a professional and potentially effective way of dealing with the situation. Finalise the SOP after receiving comments, circulate and forward to the Quality Management Department or other responsible custodian or repository administrator.

For negativity that is unavoidably brought in one's ways and causes frustration, best in that case will be to write it down, by hand. There may be little point in following up on some instances, for example if there are subtle indicators the harasser may be dealing with personal issues (e.g. at home) or even suffering under substance abuse, and this condition is transferred to the office environment. One may never know for sure. But in any event it will be helpful to record the wrongdoings and date them. Aside from possibly being able to use the record for harassment complaints and other recourse procedures at a later point, it should help on a personal level and provide relief. What's captured on paper by hand has mostly or entirely left the mind.

Needless to say, such notes should be stored in a safe place. Notes on objectional matters could also be important in performance management issues - being able to capture, track, including identifying any patterns, to verbalise and put things into perspective if need be.

Other issues

There could be subtler issues too. Some approaches, requests and the like might have their origin in occurrences from weeks or months, sometimes years back. People may, even subconsciously, wish to get back on a personal level on certain matters, on which they have been holding grudges - rightfully or wrongfully. Reading between the lines in all communications is therefore a valuable skill and many needless loops can thereby be avoided.

In this regard, if you realised that you yourself indeed wrongfully caused grief for a colleague a while ago through neglect, carelessness or inconsideration, ensure to apologize and try to rectify the underlying matter, to clear things for the future. Human decency and the responsibility to contribute to a harmonious workplace call for such rectification in any case, regardless of any particular consideration or issue.

Conversely it seems possible, at least retrospectively on reflection, that people might even be susceptible to injuries or accidents, small or big, such as sports or car accidents, due to unresolved conflicts at work and/or resisting change, with the conflicts discharging - while appearing unrelated on the surface - in such way with a certain time lag[18].

Another thinkable phenomenon could be that of some well-respected colleagues, spiritual leaders, "elder statesmen" in an organisation, emerging over time as master manipulators, who may try to exploit weaknesses, passions and drivers of staff to guide them unknowingly into conflict or misfortune, for their own benefit or even entertainment.

E.g. if one is more of an impulsive type, an emotional person, has social consciousness, is perhaps an empath, has strong ethics or seriously dislikes injustice, one might tend to act or intervene (too) quickly, or intervene on issues that are not really of one's concern, i.e. fighting other peoples' battles. This may be exploited by mal-intended colleague(s) in the

---

[18] The 2005 book by Tepperwein, Rolf *Was Dir Deine Krankheit sagen will: Aktiviere die Heilkraft deiner Seele* [What your illness wants to tell you: Activate the healing power of your soul], mvg Verlag, reprint 2017, even contains a chapter on "accidents".

background. Therefore, once recognised – an essential first step – it would be advisable to retract from such self-harming behaviour and/or relationships, incrementally but determinedly, and return to an arm's length, healthy distance and reflected consideration in interactions with such people.

Some elders or managers might also be displeased if their role as chief consolers of the team is at risk or they perceive it to be as such. While it may appear trivial, as there is of course sufficient space for human consolation in all forms, it would be good to be aware of such phenomenon and its possible implications.

Be healthily cautious also in revealing personal issues, you have a right to privacy. With a turn of events or in a different context, these may be exploited by adversaries or friends turned foe at a later stage. Harmless information about your family, relationships, associations, previous jobs, minor health ailments, financials, habits could become dangerous weapons when in the wrong hands and used with malicious intent. You have a fear of speaking in public (doesn't almost anyone ?), you have a habit of talking with your cat or plants, you have a craving for sweets, or just don't like to get up early ? Do people really need to know this ?

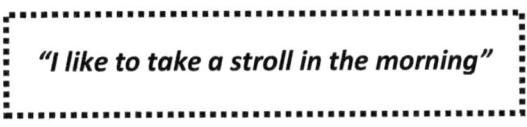

"I like to take a stroll in the morning"

Do people need to know this ?

Most institutions, organisations and businesses, in particular public entities, abide by respectable principles, are established with a noble mission, set in a good overall framework and are based on good fundamental rules and regulations. Usually all tools, resources, regulations etc. are in place to make or maintain the entity as a good organisation or system. Therefore, you can use those tools, resources, and point to or apply the rules and regulations of your organisation where appropriate. The UN is a prime example in this respect, i.e. for all instruments and structures being in place for establishing and sustaining an effective system for public good.

If/when standing up for organisational values, rightfulness, goals, there is no specific need to be afraid of controversies, presumed repercussions, not succeeding, not achieving justice at that moment and in the worst case e.g. one's contract possibly not being extended, one's post being abolished or otherwise being let go, followed by an internal review process and/or judicial procedure.

If you are doing the right thing, you will in the mid- or long-term persevere and find prosperity, happiness, and reap the fruits from your efforts, for standing up and maintaining your self-respect. Should it come to the worst and the system, i.e. internal review, oversight, internal justice system including internal court sequence, do fail the concerned, then so alas be it. But what is retained for that individual in the process are the invaluable personal assets of dignity, belief, self-respect, integrity and professional experience, which will be appreciated at other capable, intact, principled and merit-driven institutions or also as an independent operator.

Judicial processes can of course be very trying and draining for the concerned and his/her support group, and this in both personal (mental/physical) and professional respect, including even on a basic philosophical or spiritual level if the points of contention go very deep, reflecting fundamentally different understandings of life, purpose, broader goals, human interaction and human existence as such.

However, those formal processes may still be important from the perspective of achieving personal closure in regard to disagreements, allowing the individual to proceed along new paths without or with much reduced burden and liabilities from the past. And, if/when ever encountering respective colleagues or counterparts from the past, it may help in meeting those people with one's head held high, confident in both one's position and person, of having done the right thing, and hence being in the clear and at peace with oneself, one's surroundings, and one's past, present and future.

****

_____ CHAPTER 18 _____

Succeeding

What does it mean to succeed in a job ? While it is possible to attach this to specific stellar achievements, flagship projects etc., I rather believe that it's a process, and the path is the goal. Success is when you have reached a next level, be it an inner or outer level.

Steady application helps you reach that next level. And to keep in mind that excellence can also mean ensuring _absence_ of problems arising as time progresses, by diligent application and foresight.

In my view, the following are some main success factors and supportive elements, beyond those already discussed (with some exceptionally repeated):

<u>Groundwork</u>

1. Employing a fact-, evidence- and data-based approach. Check assumptions against facts and data, do not go by myths, even or especially if these have been circulating for years or decades.

2. Planning, structuring; using roadmaps, graphics, charts, tables, wherever helpful. Differentiate between short-, mid- and long-term planning.
3. Applying a modular approach, and working in manageable segments. For tedious tasks, set daily quotas, e.g. writing 5 or 10 pages per day, or reading 100 pages per day, 50 in the morning and 50 in the afternoon.
4. Distinguishing between micro and macro levels.
5. Always checking organisational and procedural responsibilities (is it your job ?) before embarking on a task/action. This may sometimes even ward off greater hazards, e.g. being "entrusted" with dangerous tasks or dispatched to hazardous locations.
6. Not permitting others to tell you how to do your job, particularly when accountability for the result remains with yourself, and the would-be instructor intends to take none such !

Practical and useful

7. Time management, prioritisation.
8. Quality vs. quantity: Identifying when one is more important than the other, and when perfect is the enemy of the good (pragmatism vs. idealism). Applying relative weighting in finite settings (e.g. resources).
9. Due diligence.
10. Running To-Do list, checklists for routine/repetitive tasks, Corrective and Preventive Actions (CAPAs) system.
11. SOPs, KPIs, metrics; Total Quality Management.
12. Thinking in gradations, thinking in-between things.
13. What gets measured gets done.

14. Just do it ! (Subject to reason and limits).
15. In innovation: Generally, what's not forbidden is allowed.
16. Use of e-tools, artificial intelligence.
17. Gathering data and making use of resources already in place, often right in front of oneself.
18. Engaging scientific support - including data science - and research as appropriate.
19. Information and knowledge sharing.
20. Use of project management tools (e.g. logframe, critical path analysis, helpful also in non-project settings !).
21. Not shying away from picking up pieces from the ground and doing other 'dredging' or 'excavation' works.[19]
22. Reading regulations, handbooks, guidelines, including the regulated exceptions, they can be helpful allies !

Abstracting

23. Being aware of functions and purpose. Always question, at least in your own mind, what the purpose of matters, actions is, e.g. the purpose of a report.
24. Similarly: awareness of form vs. function (ethics).
25. Observant observation, including of all non-action.

Strategic

26. Leading and getting to solutions by asking questions.

---

[19] The famous basketball star Dennis Rodman describes this approach in his 1997 autobiography *Bad as I Wanna Be*, Dell, reissue edition, indicating that his success in basketball was built on picking up the rebounds (missed throws), where others considered this beneath themselves.

27. Knowing when to get out of the way.
28. Turning problems into solutions. Challenges are opportunities.
29. Risk management also means maximising successes.
30. Turning diverseness into complementarity, mutual gains.
31. Use of nonviolent, non-confrontational, communication wherever possible; employing positive communication and avoiding "I" as much as possible; ("*It would be much appreciated to receive …*", "*Would it be possible to …*", "*Clarification of this point would be essential for …*", "*It's unclear whether …*", "*The report would benefit from …*").
32. Negotiating successfully. Understanding the interests of counterpart(s), finding common grounds, points of resolution; *Getting to yes*[20], best as win-win for all.[21]
33. Consider working with rewards instead of penalties.
34. In conflict management, practicing self-awareness and understanding, applying de-escalation techniques, though taking a stand as and when necessary.
35. Defending oneself in difficult situations by asking questions, going deeper, addressing details, involving technical expertise, bringing in relevant third parties.
36. Always keeping in mind the respective Mission, Strategic Goals and Plan, Workplan(s), and the greater good.
37. Stepping back to see the big picture (holistic view). E.g. effects of poverty, social determinants of health.

---

[20] 1981 bestseller by Fisher, Roger and Ury, William. E.g. (2012) new edition, Random House Business.
[21] Otherwise at least have ready to hand: *Best Alternative To a Negotiated Agreement (BATNA)*.

38. Making use of partnerships, e.g. Public-Private Partnerships, Multi-Stakeholder Platforms.

Softer aspects

39. Working in organisations means working with people and hence respect for human rights, customs, values and views.

40. Creative and active use of language: comparing meanings in different languages (semantics) to arrive at best formulations. What you cannot explain to the bus driver, your cousin etc. you have probably not fully understood or there is some other fundamental conceptual error.

Other and final

41. Among other adages: 80/20 rule (Pareto principle), focussing on value-adding matters; use of emotional intelligence (EI/EQ); cultural awareness; a journey of 1,000 miles begins with the first step; a stitch in time saves nine; nipping in the bud; staying clear of "procrastinitis"; what you don't have in your head, you have in your legs; just touch it once[22]; if you want to get

---

[22] In the sense of *"Do not look at something unless you are going to process it."*, cf. https://apex-able.com/touch-it-once-principle/https://www.cnbc.com/2018/06/21/touch-it-once-method-for-tasks-can-boost-productivity.html. However, as mentioned in Marsha Egan's website https://www.marshaegan.com/resources/articles/email-productivity-touch-rule-hows-working/ this can well be modulated to *"Touch each item no more than twice !"* or in fact my preference would be: *"Handle each item effectively only once."*, i.e. only deal

it done, give it to a busy person; thoughts and reality differ; what you see is what you get; calling a spade a spade; if it ain't broke, don't fix it; closing the barn door after the horse has bolted; teach a person to fish, you feed him/her for a lifetime; trust is good, control is better; nothing is off the record; Murphy's Laws[23] (in part); nothing succeeds like success.

42. General considerations: giving credit (recognition) and taking responsibility where indicated; consensus-based approach; active listening; dialogue; differentiating between noise and meaningful communication; understanding silence; circumspection; stoicism; effective use of resources; enabling synergies; empowerment, delegation; leading by example; openness and humility; trust and respect need to be earned; appreciation, saying thank you, exercising TLC ("tender loving care"); finding the right balance between core functions, other in-house activity and outsourcing; centralisation vs. devolution; active change management; fit for future[24]; ideas can move mountains[25]; organisational and individual agility; sustainability.

---

with it once in-depth, completing it, without needing to revisit it in its core, and limit other, auxiliary handling of it to a minimum.

[23] Cf. e.g. https://en.wikiquote.org/wiki/Murphy%27s_law and similarly also https://en.wikipedia.org/wiki/Dilbert.

[24] See e.g. https://futurefitbusiness.org/.

[25] Other brilliant quotes at: https://www.quotespedia.org/.

Figure 10 Mantras to follow at work

.

Advancing or progressing in your career means applying the principles and due diligence as covered in this book, applying best practice in your field (with exceptions of course where indicated according to your best judgement) together with awareness of its respective trends, and a drive for / vision of the future, paired with perseverance.

If you are promoted, awesome, celebrate the occasion at scale and the pay-off for your sustained dedication and diligence. Thank yourself, your support group and reward yourself accordingly. This is definitely a milestone achieved, sincere congratulations !

Yet, sadly, do not count on any such promotion. If in doubt, what you see may just well be precisely what you get.

Otherwise, therefore, when you find the time has come to advance your career, embark again on the process set out from Chapter 2 on in this book. Establish this point in the not-too-distant future, since as mentioned these recruitment processes can take up to 1 – 2 years. Do not wait for the one or other anticipated "breakthrough" project before preparing to move on. Stay realistic and reasonable, but at the same time confident and optimistic when reviewing and charting out your path, as master of your destiny. Remember, you are the boss !

****

_____ CHAPTER 19 _____

Networking

Networking can be a bit of a cliché. Of course, networking is important and essential for enabling or facilitating your work, and for progressing. This includes use of social media. A presence and interacting e.g. on Facebook, Instagram, Twitter, LinkedIn will keep you informed, open up new perspectives and opportunities, and can generally be a great source of inspiration.

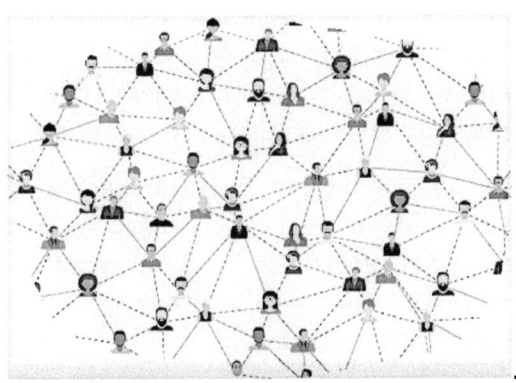

Figure 11 Networking

I would think networking is at its best when it evolves and is practised naturally, i.e. genuinely. Contacting, reaching out and interacting with genuine interest resonates maximally. People sense or will otherwise eventually be disappointed if they find there were ulterior motives in communications with them. Where a salesperson for example engages a new contact on the common interest of basketball, before then sooner or later making a pitch for a sale of a sports channel subscription or other product, is both flimsy and objectionable. If in doubt, this just leads to frustration, discontinuation of interaction, and rejection

Having an agenda in communication over social media, is also not necessary. There are scores of interesting and interested people – whether as individuals or in representing organisations/others – in the ether who are open to mutual learning, interaction, inspiration and growth. So it's not difficult, and in fact much more effective, to be genuine, rather than following any devised strategy. Therefore, my recommendation would be to be real/authentic to the greatest extent possible, and follow your natural inquisitiveness, curiosity, talkativeness and sense of connectedness. What goes around, comes around.

Your office and home can be best starting points for venturing out into the world and connecting with people. Spread your wings, and engage in all channels that resonate with you and are in harmony, or challenge you positively, with your plans and aspirations.

****

_____ CHAPTER 20 _____

"Work-life balance"

Figure 12A Work-life balance

In the past decades, this was the catchphrase, solving all problems and with which one just could not go wrong. Work-life balance is most important, agreed, but I would also agree with newer insights which advocate that work and life are present at all times, simultaneously, at any instance. A certain degree of integration of work and life is therefore both healthy and effective, life is here and now.

Just simple things such as exercising mindfulness a few times during the day already help. In the office, a walk up the stairs or a stroll in the atrium or a gaze out of the window can already be a moment of collection and calm, being in touch with oneself. Even just washing up in the restroom, applying running water to hands, forearms and face, connecting with an element of earth, can be a moment of inner connection and peacefulness.

Figure 12B Work-life balance Yin Yang

Similarly, or rather conversely, in a home office environment, those moments of collection can connect you to your purpose.

What is important is to be clear on what you expect and need in life. This is individual, but common are (cf. Maslow's hierarchy of needs, from surviving to thriving[26]): financial and other security; satisfaction and motivation at work; health; partnership, relationships; spirituality; hobbies, pastime. Set boundaries for yourself. Rest and recuperation are important

---

26

https://en.wikipedia.org/wiki/Maslow%27s_hierarchy_of_needs

in avoiding burnout. Detoxify and revitalise yourself. Reward yourself too with whatever works for you.

Mens sana in corpore sano, a healthy mind in a healthy body: bodily fitness is essential and can go long ways in helping to meet the demands of your job. Regular exercise and healthy nutrition will increase your stamina and you no longer will be plagued by those coughs and sneezes, periodic flus or similar ailments. Of absolute equal importance, or sometimes greater importance: pay attention to your mental health and take measures which work for you at earliest signs. Or better still, engage in preventive healthcare (e.g. meditation, earthing, healthy eating) and do a self-check from time to time, engage with trusted family, friends or other trusted person(s), attend seminars, events etc. and/or follow experts on wellbeing via various media. There is no doubt that mental health vice-versa impacts physical health.

Provide adequate space for training and professional and personal development, and make an effort to undergo such. Usually your workplace will offer a host of training possibilities – take advantage of them ! They will enrich you, besides adding to qualifications on your CV. Also, though it may seem counter-intuitive, if your work is very strenuous and demanding, creating a "counter-fire" at work by allocating time for training, language development etc. will actually reduce the felt work pressures. Try it, it works !

Expatriate life can be challenging: an unaccustomed culture and unfamiliar surroundings, and original friends and family are far away. If it is your first time abroad professionally, it can be both exhilarating and terrifying if you have cut most or all security cords to your home country. For myself, this was one of the biggest challenges early in my career, when I took an assignment as a freelance consultant abroad: breaking off from the social security network and established structures at home - medical insurance, unemployment insurance, pension system, family, friends, culture, food, healthcare, everything. But all was well, as it turned out to be a blessing, being most rewarding in every respect.

Severing the umbilical cord in technical respect to a system – patriotism, loyalty and other principal inner alignments can of course always remain unaffected - helps you give your optimum in your new surroundings, in every way. You will be able to excel, realise your full potential, liberate yourself from previous work-induced constraints, and thereby enable you to become a best possible and truest version of your professional and personal self. And if you are religious/spiritual, you may advance to an enhanced state of enlightenment in that experience.

Keeping a security line to a system by e.g. being deployed (seconded, on leave) with a return ticket to your original workplace and location can well subconsciously or directly detract from or prevent the improvements in life envisioned by yourself in embarking on a new journey and the success you wish to achieve by going abroad. However, this in no way would mean *not* to pursue such venture abroad as a matter of principle. Benefits still clearly in my view outweigh any such potential drawbacks. And it has happened that secondees at the end of their term abroad have decided to remain in their new found home.

The solution to the challenges faced abroad is to stay positive, remain thankful, relish the new impressions, your new freedom to explore and start afresh, and to create and nurture your own community and family of friends, associates, contacts. Find the places where you are at ease and have a sense of home.

It may be multiple places, and one of them may just be the magnificently blossoming bush outside your window with the spectacular, exotic butterflies on it. As clichéd as it may sound, home really is where your heart is.

*** Stay positive ! ***

Staying positive in unfamiliar surroundings

****

****

_____ CHAPTER 21 _____

Final words

Everyone has their own view on life, visions, dreams and aspirations, ideas and beliefs, essential motivators and drivers, principles, morals and structures. And this is good, resulting in the plurality of our being.

In regard to jobs, I have found that as important as everything may be around a profession and career – finding personal and professional satisfaction, enabling a way of living, reaching one's goals – it is equally unimportant.

Titles, functions and achievements fade in importance over the years. In my opinion, what stays and matters in my opinion are people, encounters, moments, experiences, health, spirituality, accord of body and soul. And everything happens for a purpose, and what that purpose may be may sometimes only transpire with significant time delay. But everything is for the good. So again, my recommendation is to take it easy, relax, breathe. Whatever happens and whatever you are experiencing or undergoing, be appreciative of life as you have formed it and as it comes your way, cherish the wonderful moments and celebrate the great achievements. Today, every day.

****

INDEX

Q

R

S

_____ ADDENDUM _____

Further information

If you have any questions or would otherwise like to inform yourself further, visit my website at www.xpatjobsupport.com, and my LinkedIn profile is https://www.linkedin.com/in/j-f-loeber-profile. You can also contact me at info@xpatjobsupport.com, I try to respond to all emails. As set out at www.xpatjobsupport.com, I hold online seminars from time to time, and where possible provide individual support.

==================================

(Notes)

(Notes)